Dealing W

Dealing With Fame

Frank Shapiro

Published by

Frank Shapiro

ISBN 978-0-9559331-2-7

Dealing With Fame

About The Author

An astute businessman for over twenty years Frank Shapiro, although having previous interests in the music industry became seriously involved in early 1996 when he co-founded a Music Management Company, a Recording Company and a Music Publishing Company.

Following the sale of his highly successful optical stores with over eighty employees, Frank was keen to use his management and business skills on the challenge of making his entertainment management companies major world-wide forces. So when this opportunity arose Frank was not slow to take up the challenge of signing up performers, songwriters and producers. With many years in management under his belt Frank is used to dealing at the sharp end of business.

It is not uncommon for managers and agents in the world of entertainment to push clients towards the idea of making hay while the sun shines. In other words it is often believed that there is a window of opportunity, often very small, in which to make a name for oneself and to secure the future by taking advantage of the financial opportunities that come with it.

This works for some people but for others the workload and living life in the public glare takes its toll on their life. This often leads to a downward spiral of unhappiness and unfulfilled existence. Frank noticed that some of his clients who were signed to his management company, although seemingly having it all, felt unfulfilled. From the outside they appeared to have it all; plenty of money, good looks, fame, a jet set lifestyle and adoring fans clamouring to be with them wherever they went. The distress he saw in these clients is what set Frank on the road to supporting individuals, many of them in the public eye, as they come to terms with having a private life as well as a public one, through his now well-established coaching practice. He equipped himself for the job of supporting individuals, both in and outside of the entertainment industry by training as a Life Coach. Because of his years working closely with people in the public eye, he felt well placed to give some support to those not able to deal with the pressures that their fame brought.

Frank now makes himself available to people at whichever stage of fame they find themselves; before, during or after. He recognises and empathises with individuals who feel that fame has been or still is a little hard to handle.

Frank can be contacted at frank@frankshapiro.com

Introduction

I was fourteen years old, and imagined I knew it all. I thought that my bike riding skills had finally been conquered. I had been able to ride a bike for years, but this was the day that I felt I could go anywhere and do anything with my bike. At last it was part of me and felt like a continuation of my body instead of just a piece of metal that I was holding onto.

As I built up speed to what felt like a hundred miles an hour, for the first time I was sure my bike and I were one. I had at long last got it sussed.

The main road was long, straight and an easy ride. It was busy and had lots of traffic speeding past me only a few feet away, but I was in control. I knew how to ride my bike when things were going smoothly and was confident that I could ride it in any situation no matter how difficult the road or the traffic on it became. So busy thinking about this and feeling confident about the easy ride I was having, I didn't think anything would ever happen to my bike and me. I was in control.

Then it happened. I hit the kerb. There was no apparent reason for this painfully embarrassing incident to take place, it just happened. One minute I was hurtling down the road at the speed of light then before I knew it I was off the bike and somersaulting through the air in such a spectacular way that any circus acrobat would have been proud of. My bike followed and landed a short distance away. Neither my bike nor I were damaged in any significant way, apart that is for a little scratched paintwork and a little dented pride. I got back on my trusted friend and rode home.

A few years ago I was thinking about what had happened that day; the day I thought I was invincible but wasn't. I thought about how what I learned was so much like life. I was on a journey that day. I began at my friend's house and my goal was simple, to arrive home. At the time I hadn't thought about it in this way but that was what it was, a goal.

It may be a bit of a cliché, but life is also a journey. Each of us begins our personal journeys at birth and our final goal is death. Like my bike ride we all hope we get to the final destination without too many falls.

When I fell off my bike that day, over thirty years ago, I had a choice. I could have decided to sit at the edge of the road and give up on the rest of the journey, maybe even walking the rest of the way home and giving myself a hard time over what had happened, or I could have got back on the bike and carried on the journey as planned. I chose the latter. We are presented with very similar choices during our long journey through life.

When we have a fall or a setback, we have the opportunity to choose, for whatever reason, either that we are not going to carry on in the same way as before, or we can understand that what happened was not going to hinder us from making the journey as planned and reach the goal we set out to achieve.

This book is not about riding a bike, nor is it about getting through life just so that you can claim that you have completed the journey. It is about being the very best you can be and having chosen to make your unique journey of life exactly the way you want it to be.

Being famous or at least living life in the public eye brings its own set of unique challenges. Probably the most acute being the question of how to combine your public life with having a private life. In many ways it is very easy to have one or the other. If you strive to be well known and decide that you are happy to give up much of your privacy then it is achievable and may even be quite easy, especially with so many opportunities for the ordinary person to be famous. In the same way to have a private life without fame is just as easy; all you need to do is keep your head down, get on with life and don't get noticed. The challenge comes when you try to combine fame and privacy. This can be a real struggle and making each as fulfilling and rewarding as the other can at best be difficult and at worst be a complete disaster.

In an ideal world fame shouldn't stop anyone from having a private life. We each deserve to fulfil our career ambitions as well as being a private individual. Unfortunately, we don't live in that ideal world and the price of fame often is a loss of privacy and a growing distrust or suspicion of anyone with whom you come into contact, even if they are long time friends.

One would imagine that all that needs to be done is to put on your public face when you are working or in public and be the private person the rest of the time. But even if you achieve that physical separation of your two lives, accomplishing them in your spiritual and emotional life is often more difficult.

Success is often gauged on what is achieved in a person's career. I disagree with this view. The most successful people are those who achieve what they want to in their personal life and because of that are able to have enormous success filter into all other parts of their life including their career. It is the achievement of ones own personal goals that defines success.

In this book I aim to talk to the 'whole' you, not just part. I aim to talk to the emotional, spiritual and physical aspects of your life. The journey of life for those who have succeeded in being famous must include understanding their inner self and being able to live life in such a way that their personal integrity is not diminished by their achievements in their career. In some ways having a successful career is the easy part. After all, all that is required is for you to learn to be good at something and move up the career ladder.

Having a successfully fulfilling personal life is much more challenging. There seems to be no obvious formula or definitive path to follow. That is because we are all individuals and the definition of fulfilment is different for each of us. In any job, yes even working towards being a celebrity, the structure of what must be done to reach the top is pretty well set, except of course for the lucky few who slip into it without trying. But in your personal life there is no such structure to success. Or is there?

The only rule that really works is a simple one; put yourself first. I agree that on the face of it this seems a bit selfish, and in a way it is. But unless you take care of yourself totally then you will be no good to those around you and you certainly will not have a fulfilling life.

In this book we will be looking at your values, finding

out how to get your personal needs met, how to combine being a known face with a fulfilling private life and generally moving in a direction that you want to go in.

Fulfilment, especially in your personal life can happen by accident. Many people go through life happy and content without ever planning too far in advance. But it is much more assured if you plan it and build a strong life foundation so that you give yourself the best possible chance of having all that you want.

Life can be hard, so let's acknowledge that right from the start. Most people do have their falls and setbacks, some public and some in private. Some of the time when there is an obstacle you might feel like just giving up and taking another route, an easier route. I have heard it said many times that the reason we as individuals go through difficult times is so that we can learn from these hard times and become better, stronger people. I would agree with that to some extent but I don't think that it means that we must accept that life must be a constant battle or learning process. I do not believe that the challenges are there just so we can learn. I strongly believe that if we are aware of what we can do to make the journey smoother and prepare for our life journey more effectively then we will reduce to a minimum these so called lessons.

Our journey is without a doubt about getting to the other end but it is not just about getting to the other end at all costs. As human beings our life is as much to do with the quality of the journey as it is about reaching the desired destination. Humans are different from other animals on this earth in many ways but one of the most obvious is that most humans don't just want to survive. We also want quality of life.

Few people proactively make things happen for themselves; instead, they allow situations to drive them, which will determine where life will take them. They go through life with a 'let's see what happens' attitude, hoping that things will turn out right in the end. Living life in reactive mode puts us on the defensive most of the time. Whereas living proactively creates choice.

Many people like to ponder the past especially at certain times of the year. The most popular times for this are birthdays, anniversaries, New Year and other special occasions. At times like these we often think of the events from our past and the direction of our future. As a Life Coach I often have people tell me they are not happy with where they are in life. They say things like 'my life has been directed by what others want for me instead of what I want for myself'. Some people, especially when they are famous, put up with things they are not entirely happy with just so they don't rock the boat. They miss out on what life can really offer by allowing other people or situations to control the path of their life instead of listening and acting upon what they know to be right for their inner personal self.

When my kids were young, we used to play a game. On a Saturday when we had nothing planned for the day, I would take them out in the car on a 'mystery tour'. You know the kind of thing; you go on a journey but don't know where you will end up. These mystery tours were slightly different from most, because not even the driver, me, knew the final destination. Before we left the house, we would take it in turn to write down the directions for the tour. Each of us would choose one direction in turn. So my eldest son, who was about eight at the time, might start by writing, take third left, then my other son, two years his junior, would write, fifth on the right, and so it would go on. Eventually we would have a page full of directions and none of us knew where our journey would take us.

We'd set out on our mystery tour, full of anticipation. I stuck to the directions, and we would often pass places we had never been before. As the page of directions neared the end we would all be eager to find out where we would end up. Sometimes our final destination would be in the most beautiful countryside where we'd get out of the car and have some fun. Other times the journey would come to an end in a dead-end street in the middle of town. We knew we wanted the journey to end somewhere really nice but that didn't always happen.

So many people live their life just like that mystery tour, twisting and turning and ending up somewhere they probably didn't want to be. This is a really strange concept because most of us do plan certain individual areas within our life. For example, our vacations or what car we want to buy or which house we want to live in. We plan these so meticulously, yet we rarely take the time to plan our life direction as a whole. When it comes to the big picture we tend to leave it all to chance.

I believe the majority of us can choose to take charge of our own destiny. Take a few minutes right now to think about your career and personal life. Look back over the past ten years. If you could choose then, where you would be both physically and spiritually in your life ten years later, would it be where you are today? Now picture a time ten years in the future. Where do you want to be? What plans can you make now to be sure that the directions you take and the decisions you make will be the ones to get you to where you want to be.

My hope for you is that by reading this book you will begin to take the steps in your own life that will ensure that where you are heading is where you want to be going both in your public and personal life. Have you planned for the most important journey off all; the journey of life? Or are you on a mystery tour, which could end up anywhere? Give yourself the best gift ever and make a life plan.

The Three Stages of Fame

The Three Stages of Fame

There are basically 3 stages to the fame game. The first is when a person is striving for fame. The second is what happens during fame. And the third is the dreaded, after fame stage.

Each phase probably seems like the most difficult one, especially when you are slap bang in the middle of it, but as you make the transition from one to the other it may feel as though each stage gets more difficult.

So let's take a look at some of the things that may occur during each stage.

Stage One

Striving For Fame

Before During After

Stage 1 - Striving for Fame

What is the motivation for wanting to be famous?

What is it that makes the desire to be famous so strong that some people will do almost anything to achieve it? For some it will be the excitement that being recognised for your ability will bring. But just as often it will be because of the fear of disappointing people who want fame for you. This begs the question, why do you want to be famous? Are you being pulled towards fame because you love it, or at least the idea of it, or are you being pushed towards it because of the fear of the consequences of not achieving it?

Some people have fame thrust upon them because of their natural talent or by a learned skill that people enjoy watching them do. Others seek fame and want it at all costs, so they set out to be famous no matter how little talent or skill they have.

Here is an e mail sent to me, along with my reply, which represents some of the hundreds I have received from people who, for whatever reason, want to be famous

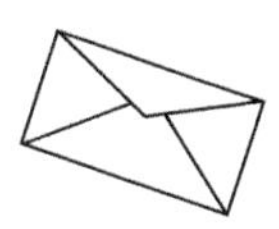

Hey Frank,

My name is James and I'm 22 yrs old. I currently live in White Bear Lake, MN on my own. My goal more than anything else in this world is to become famous but here's the kicker, I have no idea where to begin. It's so frustrating to see everyone on TV. or on stage getting all

the attention when all I want is the same thing. I'm currently attending school for business and working 2 part time jobs just to get by. Don't get me wrong, I'm a good looking guy and I love my life a lot, but I've always found myself constantly thinking about how different it would be if I were famous. A lot of people have become famous where I live such as Vince Vaughn, Josh Hartnett and Bob Dylan to name a few, but I want my chance. If you would please get back to me whenever you have time, I would very much appreciate it. I believe I need some direction as to where to start and if you could add anything on top of that, I'm here to listen. I just don't want to be thinking that life can't get better than it already is

Thanks, James

Hi James

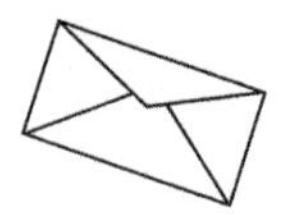

Good to hear from you.

What I do is support people who want to be, or are already famous. The thing you need to ask yourself is.... what do all the people who are famous have in common?

Is it that they can all sing? ... No.
Is it that they can all act? ... No
Is it indeed that they are all talented? No to that too.

So what is it then? Well, it is drive, dedication and determination.

Everyone who is at the top of their career (showbiz or not) is driven by one of two things

1) the pain that not achieving it will bring or does bring
2) the pleasure that achieving it will bring to them.

The difference between the people who make it happen and the ones who don't is that the pain or pleasure factor drives them forward so that every day everything they do is dedicated to achieving their goal.

So, there are often 2 stages of becoming famous
1) you must want it REALLY badly for whatever reason.
2) you must take the necessary action to make it happen.

Number 2 can be difficult. In fact it is often the

hardest time of one's life. That is where your dedication kicks in, to keep you focused.

To be honest I don't (in fact I can't) help anyone with the number 1 above; the desire to be famous. One either has that desire or not. But if you do have that all consuming desire then I can help you stay focussed as you take the actions needed to give you a shot at achieving your goal.

So what I do is, support people as they go on their own personal journey to where they want to be. In your case this is to be famous. It is about doing whatever it takes for you to make it and to be able to cope with it, if and when it happens for you.

Often we only see the end result of someone who has made it to celebrity status. We only see their life as glamorous. We don't see the fact that when others were out with friends at weekends or watching TV night after night these people were honing their skills and doing the things they needed to so as to get to where they are now.

I remember hearing a radio interview with Marty Pellow from the UK band Wet Wet Wet,

He was asked by the interviewer why he thought he had achieved success in performing and song writing. His reply was, that while all his friends were out playing football or standing around on street corners, when he was younger he was in his bedroom writing lyrics. We rarely see the build up of what makes a person a superstar until they make it happen for themselves

Many people don't make it in the entertainment industry even though they may have the drive, dedication and skills that are needed and so you must remember there is no guarantee. In fact I would go further and tell you it is probably easier to win the lotto than to become famous. But here is the thing. If you REALLY want it, then you owe it to yourself to give it your best shot. In a way you can't afford not to. There can be nothing worse than looking back and saying to yourself .... I wish I had tried .....

Remember.... if someone else in the world has achieved what you want to achieve then it is possible for you to do it too
I am here to support and encourage. If you feel that will help let me know and I can tell you more about you becoming my client
I look forward to hearing from you and well done on taking the first step towards making it

happen for yourself
Frank

One of the most important parts of what I do when I speak with people, especially young people, is to tell them as honestly as I can that they must really want the life of an entertainer.

The email I got from James and the many others I receive from people like him are often desperate attempts to get out of the situation they are in instead of a real desire to move towards the situation they are aspiring to.

Running away from your past or even your present is usually a recipe for disaster. Getting to where you want to be will be more luck than anything else if that is what you are doing. We will look at this in a bit more detail later on in this book but for now it is enough to know that you have more chance of succeeding if you are being drawn towards your goal instead of being pushed towards it by running from the situation you are in now.

Building a strong foundation

I once saw Jim Carrey interviewed on television and in amongst his zany comments and anecdotes he suddenly came across very serious when asked the following question. What motivated and drove you to achieve the fame that you enjoy today? My funnel, he said with a wry look to the interviewer, Ruby Wax, it's all down to my funnel

He went on to explain his strange statement by telling the story of his great desire to be a famous actor. As a younger man, he remembered that, as an out of work aspiring actor, how he used to take himself off as often as he could to the edge of where all the big successful stars live in Beverly Hills. He would get out of his car and stand where he could see all the big houses and outstretch his arms upwards in the shape of a funnel. He would then just stand there, arms raised and imagine that all this was being funnelled into him. He imagined himself as a funnel with his arms a giant collector of all that he wanted in life. Rightly or wrongly, that was fame. He would do the same thing in front of the famous Hollywood sign high up in the Hollywood hills.

This sounds a bit strange does it not? Or does it? I would suggest that this kind of 'funnelling' works very well. To have such a strong desire to have the things that you want in your life is fundamental to actually getting those things. What Jim Carrey was doing was exposing himself to the very things that he wanted in his life. It is similar to what some faith healers do when they help people recover from illnesses. They imagine that the illness inside the body is being destroyed.

Whether you agree or disagree with that method of healing, for whatever reason it seems to work in some cases. It certainly did for Mr Carrey when it came to his desire for fame.

Now, I am not suggesting that this alone is what made him the successful actor he later went on to be, I am sure his talent had something to do with that, but it is in his makeup to feel strongly enough about achieving what he wanted, that gave him the mind over matter determination to actually think his way to achieving his goals. This, along with hard work and talent, is what sorts out those who achieve from those who don't.

Shortly after hearing Jim Carrey make this tremendous admission of funnelling, I tried it myself. I had some turmoil in my life at the time and decided that what I wanted was peace. I had, as many have done who seek quiet times, gone for lots of walks in the countryside and along a beach. This is great and often helps clear one's mind. But what I wanted this time was something different. I actually wanted something; inner peace.

Often when we want inner piece we are not being true to ourselves. It is not actually the peace that we seek. No, what we really want is for the problems we are experiencing to disappear. So instead of seeking inner peace by hoping that things would disappear in my life I decided to look for inner peace in a more proactive way. I would actually try to funnel this peace into myself.

I drove myself out of the town where I lived and into the countryside and found myself a place that looked and felt calm. I stood there in a large open field on a lovely warm sunny day and opened my arms wide to the sky telling the universe that I wanted peace to come into my life. I imagined that the peace of the world and the stillness of that day were being channelled towards me. Call me mad or even sad but I can tell you now that I could actually feel a sense of peace overpowering me. It was a truly amazing experience.

I did this once or twice more and although it did not make the problems I was having go away, it certainly gave me the peace, desire and energy I was looking for which helped me deal with them.

Jim Carrey did his funnelling exercise often apparently. He continued to welcome in the things he felt he wanted in his life by searching for them through his mind. He honed his talent through hard work and a determination to perfect his personal style of acting.

Before the famous become famous it is vital, if they are to have any chance of having some kind of normality in their private life, to have certain things clear about themselves. These will include:

- Sorting out their own personal values
- Making sure they know about how to get their needs met
- Being well protected
- Having great daily habits
- Investing in their personal life
- Setting up strong personal boundaries
- Understanding their personal standards and how these impact on others
- The art of attraction
- How to handle other people

- Looking after their body, mind, spirit and soul
- Acknowledging that they have choice in everything they do (remember you have it too)
- Making sure that a fulfilled life is their goal not fame itself

This is an e mail I sent to a 24-year-old who contacted me. She was already on the fringes of entertainment success and wanted more but she had a fiancé and felt pulled by the dilemma of wanting to pursue her career as well as having a normal family life. She wanted to be true to herself and also honest with others. We had been talking for a few weeks before she wrote me this e mail about what she was going through and the guilt she was feeling about her personal desires which may actually be at odds with having a 'normal' family life.

Hi Fiona

Great to hear from you.

I arrived home safe thanks.

This is quite a long e mail Fiona so bear with it. I hope it will help you in the very foundation of making this happen for yourself. You might want to print it off and really think about what I say here. It is not often that I meet someone who I really want to support for no real reason. I do work with people who are starting out but mostly I work with people who have already 'made it big' in their chosen field. I am offering my support to you if you want it. My job is not to get you jobs but to get your mind and attitude correct so that you can make your dreams happen for yourself. Your future is in your own hands..... Scary but true! I saw you with people and I saw you on stage..... I truly believe that you have the beginnings of what it takes to have a successful career as an Actor.

Now it is up to you. I must say I really enjoyed meeting with you and to hear the dreams you have for yourself is exciting. It might be hard for you to understand this but I know exactly where you are at right now in your life. I have worked with people who have similar dreams. I know you want to achieve your own personal career dreams but don't want to upset the applecart in your personal life. I want you to realise that this is totally understandable. I understand that you have needs as an individual that possibly will conflict with what the entertainment industry may throw at you should you become really successful, as well as the pressures you will face on your way to being successful.

I know that you probably want to 'have your

cake and to eat it', you want the best of both worlds. There is nothing, absolutely nothing, wrong with that. But to make that happen successfully you must follow in the steps of those who already combine their personal and public life successfully. There are however many in the industry who are not able to balance life and career and at best are successful in one or other and at worst fail at both. The career in entertainment that you so badly want often turns out not to be very compatible with settling down and having a regular family life. But there is a way to have it all.

I work with a lot of successful people in the industry and I have also worked with many who never make it. Believe it or not it has little to do with talent and lots to do with attitude but in the end it has everything to do with honesty. Of course one needs the level of talent to get you the jobs you want and one always needs to seek help in improving that talent (acting, singing, presenting) but the very first step is honesty.

By now I am sure you are saying ... what on earth are you talking about Frank? Well let me tell you what I mean. The first and most important step you will ever take for yourself is to be honest in 2 areas. Firstly, Honesty with yourself and secondly, honesty with those you are closest to and love.

Being honest with yourself.... Ask yourself what you REALLY want for yourself in your career and also in your personal life. Don't be wishy washy or vague and say something like 'I want to be successful and happy.' Be focussed in what you want for yourself. It might be something like 'I want to be presenting children's TV by April' or ' I want to have a solo spot with a touring company by September' or ' I want to be regularly working in theatre by December' or ' I want to be married by February.' You get the idea? Then you need to ask yourself why you want these things. Be honest once again because unless you know your real motives and are honest with yourself about them then it will all fall apart eventually. You might want these things for yourself because of the attention they will bring or because they make you feel sexy or that they will make you wealthy or that you want to show people back home that you can make it or ... or ... or.....

This is being honest with yourself. Then once you have worked all that out for yourself and

you are sure that you are being 100% honest about what you want and not just dreaming or wanting it because of any other outside influences then it is time to tell those closest to you and those who can help you achieve it, whatever it is you want.
Ok so those closest to you. Your boyfriend, tell him honestly about your dreams and goals. Tell him firstly about your own personal dreams as an individual then about the ones concerning the two of you as a couple. It is vital that you remain an individual within the relationship for you to be fulfilled and successful as a human being, which will help you be fulfilled as the partner of your boyfriend fiancé, husband. Then share your dreams with your CLOSEST friends and family who will support you.

No need to go too deep with them. It is vital that you tell those around you what you need from them, support, love, understanding, patience. Tell them that you do not want or need them to be critical of your dreams and goals.

Tell them this as it is important for you to be only surrounded by positive people.

About your dreams. You must live them every day, just as I said to you when we spoke before.

Talk to everyone as if it is an interview for TV. Or when you are on stage, perform as if it is for an audition.
Let the real you shine through in everything you do. I am sure you have a side to your personality that few people ever get to see. Let it out in everything you do.

In your e mail to me you set out a few things you want to do and a few people you want to talk with. That is great. The time scale you are talking about doing these things in are reasonably long term which gives you time to ponder the things I am asking of you in this e mail. I will always be honest with you Fiona and from some of the things you have said to me, I believe that possibly the main thing that drives you is fear.....

Fear often drives us forward but let me suggest to you the best way to succeed.... do what you do in the future (both in personal life and career life) because you love it, because you want it, because you cannot live without it..... not because you are fearful of the consequences of not achieving it. You talk about doing work with your local touring company.... is that what you really want or is that a stepping stone? Does it just seem a reasonably easy way to be on stage and be with your man or is it what you really want to do? I ask this so that you will consider whether this is a halfway compromise and will keep everyone happy (except you)

Be honest when you answer that question Fiona. It is vital you are honest. What you tell yourself is totally secret. So be open and honest about why you feel that is the way to go. Will it get you closer to presenting your own TV show and acting? Be focussed on what YOU want for YOU. It will make you a more fulfilled individual which will make you a better partner/fiancé/wife.

Of course I will look over the letter you want to send to the touring company. Send it on to me.

On your relationship with Tom. Fiona, there is no doubt that any change of direction in either of your careers, because of what both of you do, will probably put a strain on your relationship. It would with any relationship. More so for you two because of the industry you are both in. This again is where you need to be honest with yourself. You must not become 'needy' in the relationship. You must not need Tom in your life in order for you to be happy. A partner should add happiness to your life, not be responsible for making the other person happy. Of course you want him in your life and he adds to your happiness. But you must be happy as an individual or your relationship will suffer anyway. The biggest piece of advice I can ever give you is to be a fulfilled individual within the relationship.

At some stage you will need to choose what takes priority in your life. Not necessarily that you will need to choose between a partner or your career but between smaller things like, choosing between taking jobs that will mean you are apart for a while or not. Whatever you choose you must choose because you want that particular thing and not because of the fear of losing the other thing.

These are big issues and some deep honest thinking is called for Fiona. I see too many people do what they do and have a glamorous life which outsiders think must be great but within themselves many are totally unfulfilled. I also see people with a wonderful marriage but inside they are cut up about the fact that they had to give up being themselves to have that. Having both is possible but first (and this is why I have said what I have said in this e mail) you need to build a strong personal foundation and know yourself inside out so that you are living life as your authentic self.

No one can make it happen for you or make decisions for you but those around you can offer support as you move forward to having all that you want in life. I want you to succeed in entertainment if that is your desire but even more importantly I want you to succeed as a human being.

Frank

Love To Be Famous

There is no doubt about it, fame can and often does destroy a person's soul so that he or she becomes unrecognisable to those who once knew them.

The once ordinary person full of ambition and happiness becomes like a stranger to themselves. What I mean by that is that their values, morals and standards often change which makes them unrecognisable to those round about them and to themselves. Sometimes the physical appearance looks the same as before and may even improve for a short time, but that inevitably changes too.

There are however others who thrive on being famous and blossom every time their ego is massaged and encouraged by those around them. It doesn't seem to matter who it is that encourages them or even if they are too sincere. Friend or complete strangers, they all help to feed the self image. Those people who grow personally as a result of their celebrity are normally the ones who are in the fame game for reasons other than just to be famous. These people are almost without exception the ones with real talent for what they do.

The actor, for whom fame is the only motivation for acting, usually allows the realisation of their ambition to change their core being which allows a monster to develop. Never satisfied, always striving for more and never fulfilled with the success they have achieved, these are the people who often end up in the front pages of the tabloids for all the wrong reasons.

On the other hand the actor whose love for acting is the

driving force is recognised because of the talent he or she has. This gradually and without forcing it, automatically allows their once private life, to become a public one, and they are in a much better situation to handle their success.

There are good reasons why fame affects these two sets of people in different ways. For one, they have different motives for wanting the same thing. The actor who, through his or her talent has their skill recognised, has a choice. The choice is, do they remain a great, locally recognised, stage actor in a small West End theatre or do they go for the big time by putting themselves up for international films? Choosing the first will allow them to do what they love doing while having a certain amount of privacy outside their local community. While choosing the other route will see their private life disappear forever. This 'choice' stimulates thinking. Thinking stimulates self questioning and questions result in reasoning. It is this process, culminating in reasoning that allows sufficient self-examination as to their motives, leading to their eventual decision.

So, we come back to choice. This person has, after consideration chosen to pursue his or her career knowing that the eventual outcome could possibly result in their private life being less private.

Those who seek fame with the sole intention of being famous are chasing something which is not within their own power to control. Choice, hence reasoning, has been taken away from them. The decision as to whether this person will achieve their goal and become famous will, if there is little or no talent, at best be pure luck and almost certainly be at the mercy of the media and the whim of the public.

Having choice and being prepared for what might happen should one become famous is an important part of how fame affects individuals. This is worth remembering should it ever come knocking at your door.

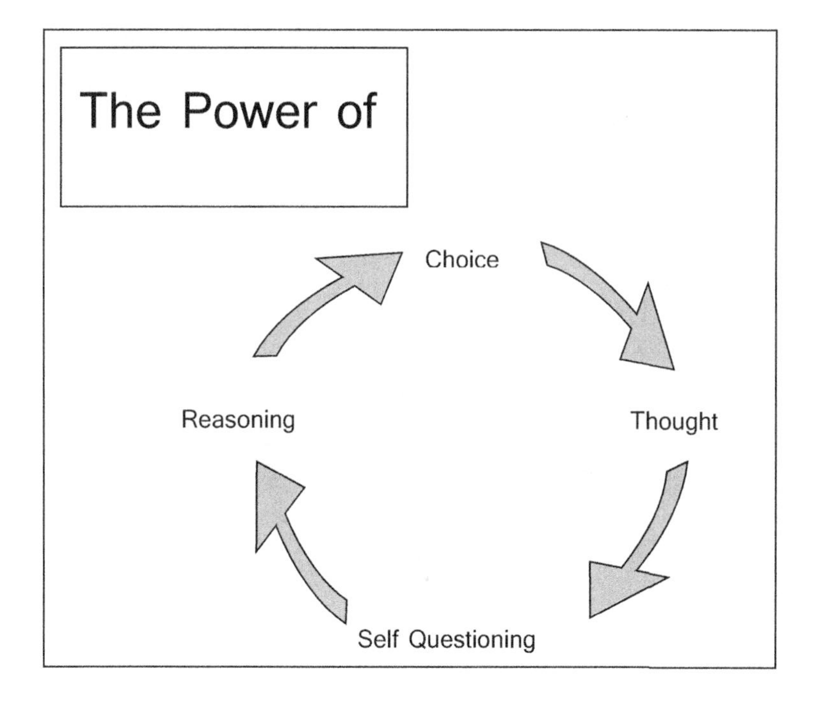

Rejection

None of us enjoys being rejected. For most of us rejection happens in a relatively private and reasonably safe environment.

From the insignificant rejection of a potential date refusing to give you his or her phone number, to the more significant rejection of people you may want to be friends with growing up, or the more difficult rejection of being an abandoned child, in the main our worst rejections will normally, no matter how devastating, at least be in private.

Think of a time when you felt rejected in your life and remember the negative feelings that followed. Now imagine that had happened and you suddenly found that it was front page news. Having your rejection made public means that you cannot hide it away until you are ready to deal with the hurt you felt. No, when your rejection is public you are forced to deal with it there and then, whether you are ready to or not.

Rejection will almost certainly happen to every public figure at some point in all three stages of fame; before, during and after. Yes, rejection happens to people even when they are huge celebrities. You can feel rejected by friends, the media, fellow celebrities, and your fans.

Rejection isn't confined to those who seek or have achieved celebrity status, it is almost certainly part of the life of just about every human being no matter what they do or who they are. However, rejection, hard as it can be to come to terms with, is not the overriding factor here. The important thing is how you choose to deal with it.

A good understanding of yourself and your abilities is vital for you to be able to overcome the negative feelings that come with rejection.

Being rejected and for that matter being praised, is part of life, no matter if you are famous or not. Rejection tends to become a way of life, especially in the early stages of public life.

Politicians are typical of a group of people who are either personally rejected as individuals or have their ideas and policies rejected by their peers or the public they serve. It becomes a way of life for most politicians, having to stand up for themselves and fight their corner on a regular basis. They are voted in at the height of their success and pushed out of office when things go against them. And all this is done on a world stage.

It doesn't need to be all bad though. Understanding rejection and accepting that you are able to deal with it is a big part of the self improvement process. It helps shape who you are and often strengthens your resolve.

The feeling you get from being rejected is an emotion. Understanding your emotions, not only the ones resulting from rejection, helps us accept ourselves for who we are. Never deal with your emotions by pretending they don't exist. Acknowledge them, try to understand them and become stronger because of them.

Remember, nothing that happens to you either by way of an event or the actions of another person, need affect you in a significant way. How you deal with these external situations is what makes the difference to your personal journey. You can learn to choose to allow negative things to affect you or not. This is what ultimately helps or hinders you throughout life.

By taking time to understand yourself through your emotions you remain in total control of your own physical and spiritual destiny.

Life is the goal not fame

When you focus on only one thing in life no matter how big or important you think it is, then you will most likely be disappointed or unfulfilled when you achieve it.

Life is the ultimate goal and each goal along the way, including striving to be famous, is only a stepping-stone on the way to achieving a fulfilled life. Just as getting your dream job or meeting a life partner may be a step in the right direction for you to feel that you have the life you want. None of the small successes you achieve during your life can possibly fulfil you on its own. They probably will feel great at the time and it is important that it takes place, but each one, along with all the other stepping stones along the way will form part of the great journey.

Each time you achieve something in your life it is as if you are cementing another brick in your great wall of life.

Each brick re-enforces the others, which are already in place, each one going toward making your whole life substantial and strong. The stronger your wall of life, the easier it will be for you to deal with any problem or challenges that you come up against along the way. Pinning all your hopes on one thing and hoping that it will, on its own bring fulfilment, will end in disaster whether you achieve it or not.

When a person rushes into a new situation without first having the strong life foundation (the wall of life) then he or she will constantly be trying to rebuild and patch it up as they go along. They will soon find that they are spending more time fixing what is wrong in their life than forging ahead with having the life they want.

Eventually most of us realise that the only way forward is to stop trying to patch things over and consider rebuilding from scratch.

Start by writing a mission statement for your life. Not just part of it but all of it. Write a few sentences that sum up what you want your life to be all about; not just part of it, all of it.

When one of my clients found this difficult to do in her life I suggested the following.

We all understand the concept of 'what would you like written on your gravestone' By asking someone this question we are asking them to look back on their life after they were dead and to best sum up, in just a few words, how they would like to be remembered.

A mission statement for life is similar to this but instead of waiting until it's all over to sum it up, you look forward and plan. At the end of your life you cannot change anything that happened during it, but today you have the opportunity to start afresh and shape the future in any way you choose.

Stage Two

During Fame

Before **During** After

Stage 2 - During Fame

Handling Fame or Not

Some of the major differences between people who are at ease with their fame and those who are not are as follows:

A person who handles fame well will tend to be secure as an individual. A person who does not handle fame well will tend to be insecure and needy.

A person who handles fame well will tend to have a good support team around them (professional and social). A person who does not handle fame well will tend to have a poor support team and attract lots of 'hangers on'.

A person who handles fame well will tend to want fame and success for their own pleasure and satisfaction. A person who does not handle fame well will tend to want fame in an attempt to please other people (including pushy parents) and for the adoration it promises to bring.

A person who handles fame well will tend to be living 'Who' they really are. A person who does not handle fame well will tend to be living 'What' they think they should be.

A person who handles fame well will tend to be living the reality of their own life. A person who does not handle fame well will tend to be living a fantasy life (the common idea of what fame is like).

A person who handles fame well will tend to be living in the present and building for the future. A person who does not handle fame well will tend to be living only for the present with no focus on the future.

A person who handles fame well will tend to have the ability to identify their needs and have them met. A person who does not handle fame well will tend not to have identified their needs so is always trying new things and be constantly searching.

A person who handles fame well will tend to be confident. This comes from an internal position. A person who does not handle fame well will tend to be aggressive. This comes from an external position.

A person who handles fame well will tend to see the past as what shapes their future. A person who does not handle fame well will tend to allow the past to dictate their future

A person who handles fame well will tend to attract fame towards them. A person who does not handle fame well will tend to always be hunting and searching for fame.

A person who handles fame well will tend to enjoy fame and be satisfied each step of the way. A person who does not handle fame well will tend to overindulge in fame and never be satisfied.

A person who handles fame well will tend to have a great quality of life no matter what they are doing at the time. A person who does not handle fame well will tend to have a poor quality of life.

A person who handles fame well will tend to have a fulfilling lifestyle. A person who does not handle fame well will tend to be unfulfilled in everything they do.

A person who handles fame well will tend to be focused on life and be alert. A person who does not handle fame well will tend to be focused on lifestyle and be distracted.

A person who handles fame well will tend to be very attractive. In other words they attract friends and sponsorship easily. A person who does not handle fame well will tend to be unattractive. People and sponsors will avoid them or want to be around them for the wrong reasons.

A person who handles fame well will tend to have some control over the media and use it to their advantage. A person who does not handle fame well will tend to be controlled and manipulated by media.

Living the 'Who' and not the 'What'

No matter what position you hold in this world, be it The King or Queen of Great Britain, the President of the USA or the biggest named celebrity in the world, you are still just an individual. You were born of woman, and you will die like the rest of us, mere mortals. You eat, sleep, breath and share the same emotions that most other people have.

In the wee small hours when all the drama and excitement of being a celebrity diminishes, those who have reached the heady heights of stardom are still the same individual beings as when they were born. Just like you and I, they are simply another individual living out their life on this place we call earth.

In the privacy of their own homes they like to watch the same things on TV, have their favourite food for lunch or cuddle up at night with their favourite teddy, just as they did before the celebrity they now enjoy had fully taken hold. Basically, deep down they are the same people now as they were before they were famous. It is simply that circumstances have altered and people now recognise them for the work they do. Without being too morbid, the saying that you are born alone and you will die alone is very true. So the fact remains that during your life you are ultimately a single individual no matter how many people you have around you to treat you like an idol.

You still have individual needs and values, likes and dislikes, fears and emotions. Dreams and goals have not suddenly disappeared from your life just because you are now famous. In fact in most cases success pushes you on to want even more success.

Living 'Who' you are, is living your true authentic self no matter 'What' you or others perceive you to be. The people who manage to have a fulfilling private life as well as a successful public life are the ones who remember this and choose to live life as the 'who' and not the 'what'

I am sure some of you, like me, are at an age where you meet people from what we sometimes refer to as 'a past life'. A person you knew from your school days, college or a work mate from years ago for example.

"You haven't changed a bit" they say.

Well if they are making a comment about 'who' you are then they are probably correct. But if they are talking about 'what' you are then the truth is you have probably changed quite a few times since you last met.

As we pass through life we take on, and assume different identities depending on which stage in life we are at and, probably more influentially, who we are with. Our attitudes change as we learn more about ourselves, our life and the world in which we live. As we hear the opinions of other people, on all sorts of topics and issues, we form our own ever changing opinions of who we are and what life is really all about.

If I think of my own life and the stages I passed through it is quite amazing. I went through the following 'what' I am:

Frank the bump inside my mother's tummy to
Frank the new born baby to

Frank the son to
Frank the brother to
Frank the school chum to
Frank the boyfriend to
Frank the university student to
Frank the Saturday boy to
Frank the professional optician to
Frank the husband to
Frank the dad (twice) to
Frank the single man to
Frank the music manager to
Frank the public speaker and writer to
Frank the life coach to
Frank the .... and so it goes on

What I am really saying here is that life is never static and as we pass through it we realise just how fluid it actually is.

People introduce us by using a whole host of different titles and often think of us as that title instead of who we really are.

Is your identity WHAT you are and what other people think you are? Or is your identity WHO you are and who you want to be? The biggest challenge you will have when you are public figure or a well known celebrity is to remember the difference between who you are and what you are.

Above I jotted down a few stages of 'what' I went through and here I list some of the attributes of 'who' I am

Encourager, creative, inquisitive, passionate, honest ....

And so the list goes on.

'Who' you are usually lasts for ever and can even be seen in you as a child while 'what' you are will depend on the stage in life in which you find yourself.

As soon as you start to think of yourself as 'what' instead of 'who' you are on the slippery slope to self destruction.

There goes; Johns' wife, Toms' dad, Bob the milkman, Jane the lawyer, Amanda the actress, Phillip the writer ....

It can even get more detailed than that, especially if you are an actor. You might end up taking on the identity of someone you portray as an actor for an extended time. Many actors and actresses find it virtually impossible to break away from a strong character they have played in a movie or a popular television series. Their career suffers as they become typecast, but their private life can suffer too as the public feed the feeling of this double life by referring to you as the character instead of as yourself.

Are you living the 'WHAT' instead of the 'WHO'?

One way to find out is to look at all the things you have enjoyed doing throughout your life so far. Look for a pattern and explore the times when you lost yourself in what you were doing. When you find a common thread, ask yourself if it continues no matter what stage in life you are going through. When you find things that are always to the forefront of your life then you are discovering the essence of who you actually are.

Is your whole identity lost because you have taken on the role of dad, mum, milkman, lawyer, wife, husband, son, daughter or dependable neighbour, minister, TV/Film character? Have you lost or forgotten the individual you really are?

It may be that you have taken on an identity that is not so obvious to you. You may have taken on the characteristic of being too serious; "There goes Debbie she is always serious"

Or that of the village funster; "William is always the life and soul of the party"

Linda the carer …. David the bully …. Sam the pushover. You get the idea.

It is possible, that because you are perceived by others to be a certain type of person, that you will start to see yourself as that type, and your identity will change in such a way that you actually believe that it is the real you. Instead of your life being shaped by your character your character is shaped by your life.

Over time you may look back and ask yourself, how did I turn out to be so negative, so aggressive, so timid, so fearful so negative, so ………

Search for the 'WHO' in yourself. Is there a party animal inside that timid exterior? Is there a caring person lurking within a brash facade? Is there a writer inside an actor? Is there a family man inside that confirmed bachelor? Is there a director inside that camera operator?

Do you want to be the person you know you really are but can't?

Can't, Yes, that's right CAN'T?

Why not?

The reason that many people feel they can't show

themselves to be the person they know they really are, is because they feel it isn't what people expect them to be. This can sometimes be the only thing holding you back from being who you know really are. It feels safe not showing the real you. It feels easier just to take on the role of what people expect from you.

Sometimes we allow tradition, even tradition which has only established itself a short time ago, to get in the way of expressing ourselves fully. What starts off being a statement ends up being a lifestyle.

I once knew a man who always wore a bow tie to work. In fact I have never, to this day, seen this chap without a bow tie on, not even at informal events. As I grew to know him better I asked him the story of the bow tie. When I asked him about it he would be in his mid forties. He said that when he was at university in his teens and early twenties he wanted to stand out from the crowd and thought that by wearing a bow tie it would help him do that. He was right, it did, but what he didn't realise was that by not reverting back to himself after he left university he had carved out an identity for himself which was not in line with who he really was. He had reduced his identity to a mere symbol; a bow tie.

"I would love to get rid of this burden" he once confided in me. "But I can't. What would people think"? What had happened was that the bow tie had defined his character and he felt it much easier to continue to wear it that to have to explain to everyone he met over the next few years why he had stopped wearing the bow tie. And in some respect he probably enjoyed being asked why he always wore it.

Are you tied (excuse the pun) to something that you know is not really part of you? What is stopping you from moving away from the things to which you know you have no affiliation?

Look back at the list above of my own 'what' identity shifts as I progressed through life. Do you notice what stays the same in each one? Yep, you got it; I am always Frank. And as Frank I can be whatever and whoever I choose to be no matter which stage of life I am at.

Do the same as I did above. Make a list of 'what' you have been throughout your life. Take your time. After you have completed the list, ask yourself if any of the things you have noted down feel in line with 'who' you really are. Is there a common thread that runs through each stage or are there some which felt perfectly in tune with you as an individual?

Find your true identity and show it to the world.

Surprise a few people today.....Let them see the REAL you.

Dealing with the Fans

This is always a tricky one. On one hand you need them, especially at the beginning of your career. But when fame takes its grip, fans, especially the obsessive ones, can really create a unique challenge for the unprepared celebrity.

Fans think they are your friends. Why shouldn't they? After all you and your publicity machine have invested a lot of time, money and energy making sure the public get to know all about you. You want them to feel close to you; you want them to associate themselves with you in the hope that they will buy your product or go and see your latest film. In an attempt to get the public to buy into you, you not only give them details about your career but you are usually happy, in the beginning at least, to divulge information about your personal life too. You want your picture to be on the front pages of all the glossies and are eager to give interviews about your likes and dislikes as well as a host of other snippets of personal information. Some celebrities take great pride in inviting the television cameras into their homes and lately seem pleased to have them there 24/7. In an attempt to woo your fans you may even be tempted to allow the media to capture the good the bad and the ugly about your life by taking part in 'fly on the wall' documentaries.

So why shouldn't the fans think of you as their friend? They probably know more about your personal life than they do about their real friends.

The problem is that 'real' friendship is a two way street. I know as much personal information about my best friend as he knows about me. He calls me on the phone as much as I call him. We enjoy each other's company and choose to spend time with each other. Friendship is mutual, it is never one sided. But this cannot be said about the relationship fans have with you the celebrity. This relationship is totally one sided, and the really strange thing is that the fan often genuinely forgets this important fact and wants you to recognise them and know all about them just as they know all about you.

After all, they paid dearly in time, money and energy getting to know you over the years, encouraged by you. Fans think that they have a right to expect you to know and care about them in a way that crosses the line between fan and celebrity. They feel that you should be as interested in their life just as they are in yours.

This is where clearly knowing from the start, who you are and what you want from your life is vital. At the beginning of your career it is so easy to give away too much information about yourself in the hope of winning the loyalty of more fans. It is important however, to make a clear definition at the start as to what you will and will not share with people who are not your true friends.

Setting strong boundaries will help eliminate problems in the future. For example, if you accept gifts from fans and acknowledge them with a personally hand written note from yourself early on in your career you are encouraging the fan to think of you as a friend. There is nothing wrong with that as long as you are willing and able to carry that through when you are not struggling for attention. They will look for this same personal attention the next time they send you something or see you at an event; in fact they will probably not only want it, they will expect it of you from that time forward.

Set up a fan club as soon as possible, even before people know who you are. If feasible get someone to go through your fan mail for you and answer all the letters on your behalf telling the fans that you have seen the letter, e mail, or gift personally and that you thank them for it. Ideally you will pay someone to do this for you but at the beginning when money is tight and there are only a few fans then do it yourself but don't let on it is actually you answering. Another great way to set up a fan club is to get one of the fans (it needs to be one that you trust and is mature enough not to be all googly eyed when you are around) to run your fan club. Usually they will do this for nothing, at the beginning anyway.

Don't lead your fans on. Give them the respect that they deserve but also make it clear from early on that you have a private life into which they are not invited.

I remember when it suddenly dawned on me how fanatical some fans can be. In fact there were two occasions. The first was when one of the bands my company looked after were on the brink of making it big. They were a pop band and the target audience were teenagers, especially teenage girls. They had just finished an afternoon interview at a radio station in Dundee, Scotland, and their security had brought the people carrier round to the front of the building. They had to walk about fifteen meters from front door to van. But instead of being a ten second walk, it turned into what could only be described as free for all battle to get them in the van safely.

We, as their management company had done our jobs well. We had built up hype about this band and as part of this hype had made public their schedule. The fact that it was a Tuesday afternoon and most of the three hundred or so kids that were waiting for them should have been at school made us realise that fans were capable of doing almost anything to get close to their idols.

The second time that I realised the impact of fanatical fans have on people in the limelight was when I stayed in a hotel for a few nights in Kensington London with one of my performer clients. We were there because he was finishing off his second album. We had not long arrived back to the hotel after being at the studio and decided to go for a drink at the bar. It was about 9.30 in the evening. At about 10.15 we both went to our rooms without having anything to eat as we had been snacking at the studio all day.

You guessed it, at about 2am my phone rang. The hunger munchies had come knocking and my client could not sleep. He wanted to go out for a pizza. Now that I was wakened I thought it might not be such a bad idea. There was a 24 hour pizza restaurant about 100 yards from the hotel and we decided to meet in the hotel lobby and walk to the eatery. On our way we noticed a couple of fans standing at the entrance of the hotel and he went over and said hi. We continued to the restaurant.

Unbelievably, by the time our pizza was served to us a bunch of about 60 fans had gathered outside the pizza restaurant. Such is the miracle of the mobile phone. It turns out that fanatical fans have a kind of secret network and take it in turns to watch their favourite stars' whereabouts and alert the rest of the team should they have an opportunity to move in. This is just after 2am in the middle of the week remember, and most of these kids were not much older than sixteen. One had even cajoled her mother into driving her and a few of her friends there. Then the resourceful fans decided they wanted pizza too and some came in to the restaurant, sat at tables close to ours and ordered food. As a parent my head was buzzing with questions; do your parents know you are out? Where do you get the money to do all of this? Why aren't you at home and in bed? These kids obviously had just one thing on their mind; to get closer to their idol.

My client shook his head, looked at me as if to say is there nowhere I can go, and walked out. As we ran back to the hotel with a gaggle of frenzied fans trailing behind us, I realised that this was life for this man. It was just an unusually odd situation for me that didn't happen too often, but for him this was his life. This was what he went through every minute of every day, and amazingly, over ten years later, is still going through.

If you are lucky, your fans will never forget you, even after your fame dwindles. If you are unlucky they will want a piece of you even when you are on your own personal time.

Your fans are important to you, without them you will almost certainly not be as successful in what you do. But they are, at the end of the day, fans not friends.

Dealing with the Media

Just like your fans, the media are one of these entities that you need but don't always want in your life. There is no doubt about it, the media, especially in the form of TV, Newspapers and Magazines are a convenient way of letting the public know who you are and what you are about. They give you the opportunity, free of charge, to get your face in front of millions of potential fans. They are, unfortunately, probably more influential in the making and breaking of your career than anything else, including your talent.

There are many examples of not so talented people getting to the top of their chosen career just because the media took a shine to them. Conversely there are extremely talented individuals who will never make it because they are not much liked by the media.

The problem with the relationship that celebrities and media have with each other is that most of the time, they both have a totally different agenda from each other. And you need to know that this is the case from very early on in your career.

Sometimes the two agendas run together in harmony but more often than not they don't.

Your agenda is that you want to have your picture and story in the paper or on TV because this brings your name and face to the fore, which in turn helps your career. The media wants your image on their product because by doing so it can increase viewing figures or can sell more papers and magazines. It's as simple as that. There is no hidden agenda or other reason for you or them to co-exist. They are quite clear about why they pester or ignore you. It is all to do with increasing sales. When they feel that having you prominently placed on their product will not increase the sales of their papers or magazine or increase the viewers on prime time television, you will not be of any more use to them and dropped quicker than you can say 'I used to be famous'

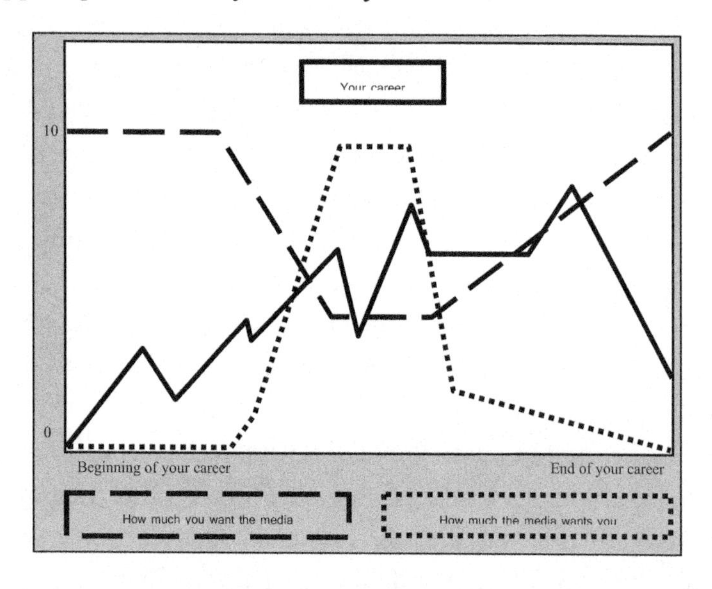

The thing that anyone in the public eye should realise is that what is a good time for you to have yourself splattered on the front cover of their magazine may not coincide with the best time for them to have you on that front cover. The timeline of the editor or producer is probably different from your own timeline. For example, at the beginning of your career when no one knows who you are, you want lots of media attention. The more attention you receive the better it is for you. You would do almost anything to get a front cover or be seen on television.

But the media don't want to know you at that stage in your career. Why should they? At that point you are simply just another aspiring wannabe.

But when you are famous and want a bit of privacy, the media are out in force. Their zoom lens cameras firmly focused on you wherever you are, whatever you are doing with whoever you are doing it with. They are trying to get a great shot of you or, if they are really lucky a shot of you looking less than your best. It doesn't matter to them which it is as either will sell their product. You are keener now to wear dark glasses and don an elaborate disguise in a bid to get away from them. And so it continues. When you need them they don't want you and vice versa.

When you find yourself in some kind of trouble either in your personal life or things are not going so well on the career front, the media are there on your doorstep. They are just as interested in your new partner as they are in your latest film. Why, because it increases their paper sales or gets them higher ratings from viewers. All you want to do is have a bit of privacy.

But who can blame them. It was you after all who kept knocking at their doors asking them to notice you and pleading with them to tell the world all about you. Can you expect them now just to ignore you?

As your career begins to dwindle and you want to make a final attempt at a comeback, the media have already turned their attention to some other, more interesting and more newsworthy person who will sell more papers for them and achieve better viewing figures.

The best way to be with the media is similar to that of your fans. You must play their game but at the same time set boundaries that both you and they can live with. Be consistent as to how much you give of yourself to them. If you invite them into your home one week, you can hardly be upset or surprise that they want that same level of exposure from you again and again. Work with the media before, during and after your career has peaked. Building a good relationship will stand you in good stead for the future when it comes to working with the media.

It has been said that the association that public figures have with the media is a love hate relationship. But remember, when you enter into such a fluctuating union it will rarely have a happy ending.

Choice Vs Need

Some celebrities, when they become famous, feel that their life is not their own and often feel trapped and out of control. Many of them explain it as feeling as if they have no choices in their life any more.

Feeling out of control when it comes to your own destiny can be a terrifying experience and will often lead to you making decisions that you would not normally make.

A while back I had a client (let's call her Mary) who felt trapped. She was not connected to the entertainment industry in any way but this true story about the situation Mary found herself in may help us understand the negative hold that feeling out of control can have on any of our lives.

Mary felt that she had no options, no choices and that she was completely trapped in a life that she didn't want to be in.

She had two children; a 6 year old boy and a 4 year old girl. Her daughter was autistic. This is a condition that really means that the child needs constant attention and has to be looked after in very special ways. Her daughter basically was not capable of looking after herself. If you saw the film "Rainman" starring Tom Cruise and Dustin Hoffman, you will remember that Dustin Hoffman played the character of an autistic man.

Mary was a single mum which I am sure you will all agree can be difficult job at the best of times, even if your children are fit and healthy. Well, she had had just about enough of her life. She couldn't see a way out of the exhausting cycle she found herself in and had no idea how she could go on looking after her autistic daughter as well as giving enough attention to her son. To add to her woe Mary had no social life to speak of and had little opportunity to develop her career or relationships with other people.

She felt trapped.

Because of her mindset Mary was sure that she had no choice other than to carry on looking after her daughter for the rest of her life. She told me that she viewed her existence like a prison sentence without any chance of escape.

The feeling of having no choice is a very powerful one, and one which can be totally debilitating. It can make a person feel that they have no life of their own and that life is hopeless and out of control. Hopelessness can often lead to depression and that was exactly where Mary was heading. Her children had become unruly because of her view of her life with them which made the kids unhappy and unmanageable.

Mary felt ashamed as she confessed to me that she resented her daughter and that she had recently begun to blame her for the lack of life she felt she had. She shouted a lot at her kids and cried a lot in front of them because she was so frustrated with her life. Her daughter didn't understand it all and her son felt left out because his mum spent so much time tending to his sister. All in all this was not a good situation for any of them.

I spoke at length to Mary about all sorts of things and asked her what she was really feeling. She told me. She said "I am trapped. I have no choice but to look after my daughter for the rest of her life".

I asked her a series of questions and the conversation went something like this:

Me — Are you telling me that you have no choice in this matter at all?

Mary — Yes that is right, I have no choice but to look after my autistic daughter and to do that I will have to give up on any hope of having a life of my own.

Me — Are you really telling me you have no choice in this matter?

Mary — Yes

Me — No choice whatsoever?

Mary — That's right, I have no choice. She is my daughter, she needs looking after so I need to look after her.

Me — Ok, so what happens if you suddenly can't look after her? I hate to even think this but what would happen if tomorrow you got run over by a bus and died. What would happen to your daughter then?

Mary — She would be taken into a special home for autistic children I suppose.

Me — Would she be well looked after there?

Mary — Yes, in fact the children in these homes are very well looked after.

Me — Ok. So if you decided you didn't want to look after your daughter anymore could you put her into one of these homes? Would they take her in even if you didn't get run over by a bus?

Mary Yes they are happy to take children in when parents can't cope.

Me So why wait until you get hit by a bus to put her in one of these special homes? Why not do it now?

Mary She is my daughter I could never give her up, I love her. She is so difficult to look after but I do love her.

Me What do you mean you could never give her up?

Mary She is my daughter, I love her and I need to take care of her.

Me Can I ask you to repeat that last sentence replacing the word 'need' with the word 'choose'

There was silence……………..

After a few moments I could hear a little sobbing

Mary I love her, and I 'choose' to take care of her

Me Yes, you are so right Mary. You see you are really <u>choosing</u> to take care of your daughter. You don't <u>need</u> to do it because there are really good places out there that could do it for you. You could free yourself from the burden right now by arranging for your daughter to go into a home. But you <u>choose</u> to look after her yourself.

There was a sudden realisation that Mary was looking

after her daughter through choice and not because she didn't have any other option open to her. This shift totally changed her attitude towards her daughter and towards her own situation. Mary was released from the feeling of being trapped in a downwardly spiralling life and changed the negative feelings into positive ones which in turn allowed her to realise every day that she had choice; to look after her or not.

Of course Mary would never give her daughter up and put her into care while she was able to look after her herself. That was not the point. And I was not suggesting she did. I was simply suggesting to her that in actual fact choice existed for her. The point was that she realised that she had the choice to do it, if she wanted to, even though she knew she would probably never actually do it.

This change in thinking made her life a lot lighter. The new feeling of lightness transferred itself to her children, especially her daughter and within a few months the relationship that the her daughter and within a few months the relationship that the three of them enjoyed with each other had changed into a much healthier one for all concerned. The daughter seemed more responsive and appeared to behave better and the son helped his mum a lot more, especially after his mum explained to him that he also could choose to help with looking after his sister or choose not to.

You don't need to have an autistic child to feel trapped in life.

No matter why you might feel trapped in any particular situation, remember that it is almost impossible to imagine a situation that you will be in where you do not have a choice.

The choices you have may not be obvious. They may not even be easy choices to make but you will have some choices in the situation you are in. Whether you take them or not is a different thing.

In this respect I suggest you ban the word 'need' from your vocabulary for the next month and change it to 'choose'

I need to visit my parents as I haven't been round for a while

I choose to visit my parents as I haven't been round for a while

I need to talk first to my partner after the big argument

I choose to talk first to my partner after the big argument

I need to ……………………………….

I choose to ……………………..

Motivation

No matter what we do in life, if we are not motivated to carry it through to a conclusion and beyond, then it more than likely will not happen.

Of course some things can happen for us or to us without us trying. There is definitely such a thing as being in the right place at the right time but for most of the time if we don't work hard and do it for ourselves it will not come our way.

Even at the height of your celebrity, if the motivation to continue on your chosen path is not strong enough then you will find it harder and harder to continue to be fulfilled in your life both personal and public.

This is when you can call on the 'who' again as referred to in an earlier chapter, and remind yourself why you wanted all this in the first place. Remind yourself that whatever it was that you wanted, which might include being famous, was not the ultimate goal but that life itself is the final goal with fame being nothing more than a stepping-stone on the way to having fulfilment.

Just as all of us are individual human beings, we each have individually different motivational triggers. By examining and understanding what these triggers are for yourself before you ever start on your journey, you will put yourself in the most advantageous position for achieving whatever you set out to do.

Ask yourself very early on in the process, what it is that motivates you and why you want to achieve whatever it is you want.

Is the driving force for you money, celebrity, adoration, acceptance or something else? There is no correct or incorrect answer to this. You cannot allow yourself to feel that it is not right to be motivated by money or adoration just because some people may think it is a poor reason for wanting something.

You have your own reasons and as long as you are honest with yourself about what they are then you will be living your authentic self. Your motivational trigger will differ from other peoples in varying degrees. It may even be a mixture of lots of different things that motivates you.

Remember also that the triggers can be physical and/or emotional. You may be motivated to getting a particular part because by doing so you will be able to afford that new car. Equally the motivation may be that by getting the part you will have proved to yourself that you actually are good enough at what you do to merit it. To complicate things even more, it may be a mixture of the two. By getting the part you will be able to afford the new car which will allow you to feel great about how you live and your lifestyle.

It is important to understand your own motivation for doing what you do and wanting what you want. That way when things get tough you can get yourself back on the road by remembering why you wanted it in the first place.

Continue to reassess your motivation for wanting whatever you want. Often when you have achieved what you want and the trigger has been satisfied then the will to push further reduces dramatically. It often helps to look beyond the actual thing that motivates you and focus on the benefits that having it will bring. For example, you may want to break into films and your motivation for wanting this is that it will give you the money you need to maintain the standard of living that you want. If then you do break into films and you are being asked to do more and more films, you may find yourself bored with it unless you remind yourself that this is what gives you the lifestyle that you want.

Your trigger is what drives you onto bigger and better things.

For example, your motivational trigger may be financial. You go for interviews and auditions through the necessity to pay bills or because you want a smart car or fancy jewels or a bigger house. When you have these things it is not uncommon for you to become unfulfilled and complacent. What is needed now is for you to think creatively.

What will having this financial security allow you to do that helps your true self to shine? It may be that you may want to give some of your wealth to good causes, to help a friend in need or to rebuild your childhood school. Think beyond the pleasures that your trigger can bring you, and focus on the pleasure you will have by doing what you want with it.

Many successful people have started off wanting what they want for personal reasons and then as they achieve their goals one by one their triggers change as they begin to realise that they can actually make a difference to other people by continuing to push themselves forward.

I am not sure that Bill Gates was motivated in the beginning by the idea that he would be able to set up a charitable foundation and help less privileged people by sharing his wealth. As he moved forward, achieving each of the goals that he set out to, he realised that he could do more with his wealth and status than he thought. It is possible that helping others is now one of his motivational triggers.

Find ways to stay focussed and so remain motivated. Gather people you trust around you so that you have a support group? Make sure you have people around you with whom you are able to talk over your waning enthusiasm. Find a place that you can go to that feels special to you. Visit this place when you need to refuel your energy levels.

Take whatever time you need so as to give yourself the space to rekindle an past vision or set yourself a new one; an even bigger and better one than before.

Balance of Private and Public life

Below are outlines of the lives of two people. Once you have read them decide which you think has the right attitude to leading a healthy, balanced and fulfilling life.

Jane is well motivated. She visits the gym three times a week for a religious workout. She is an actress and is totally dedicated to her career. Because she enjoys looking her best she eats all the right food and generally looks after her physical appearance and takes pride in her high level of fitness. Each evening Jane goes home to her husband and children. Her home life is very stressful. Her kids complain they hardly ever see her and over the years she feels her husband is not as attentive as he once was. They argue a lot and rarely talk about the future.

John has a wonderful family life. He dotes on his wife who is expecting their first child. He has an extended family that care for both him and his wife enormously. They laugh a lot and have many playful times together. At work John struggles in his commitment to the job. He secretly knows that he does not give as much to the company as his colleagues do. His thoughts are that this is why they all seem to be getting promoted over him. He would love to go on these long trips abroad with the other members of the touring cast but turns them down because of his devotion to his family. After all if he were to go away for long periods of time then his family life would suffer.

Have you decided which of these two people have the perfect balance in their life? I am sure you have guessed the answer; neither of them.

Jane is so focused on her career and on herself that her relationships with those she loves is taking a back seat and suffering because of it. John is exactly the opposite. He is so wrapped up in his family that his career is not what it should be and his fulfilment level is low.

Balance is vital for fulfilment. There is nothing fulfilling about having a great career and a lonely or unhappy existence as a human being because of a less than successful personal life, or vice versa.

The amazing thing to remember is that you can actually have it all. You can have a fantastic home life as well as a great career. How do I know that this is possible? Well one of my fundamental beliefs in life is that if someone else has achieved something, anything, then it is possible for everyone else to have too. All it takes is for you to look at yourself, be honest with yourself and understanding that deep down the life you have is not the one you set out to have. Then, and this is the part that so many people don't do and so don't succeed, you must do whatever it takes to fix the problem and go for what you want.

Your career does not define who you are. No matter what your job is it does not define you. The person who happens to be a bank manager or a teacher is not defined by his or her profession. Remaining a strong individual with a unique character is essential if you are to have the balance in life that will bring fulfilment. You must get to know what your needs and wants are in life and understand the key issues that affect you as a person.

One of the most important things not to do if your life is lacking balance is to put your head in the sand and hope it all goes away. Believe me it won't. Just like the imbalanced tight rope walker at a circus, who allows one side of the long balancing pole he is holding to get too low, you will eventually fall off.

It may help to talk to those involved in your life and tell them that other parts of your life also need your attention. You will be amazed at how supportive people who love you can be. Most people want you to be your best and to be totally fulfilled in what you do. One of the reasons they want this for you is because it makes you a better and easier person to get along with. When you are happy and fulfilled in every part of your life then the people with whom you interact will feel the benefit.

Relationships and Fame

When you are in the public eye for whatever reason then the relationships you have with other people will usually fall into four main areas.
Your relationship with yourself
Your relationship with other famous people
Your relationship with non-famous people
Your relationship with your intimate partner

Relationship with yourself.

If there is one thing that every individual can do for themselves so as to allow them the best chance of total life fulfilment, it is to make sure that the relationship you have with yourself is a great one.

Life, when it comes down to it, is all about having such a great relationship with yourself that you are able to function in the world in a positive and proactive way. If you do not have a great relationship with yourself then you cannot successfully have one with anyone else on any level. I know that sounds pretty rigid but it must be true. For any of us to have a positive and healthy relationship with anyone else, be they friends or intimate partners, we must first get the relationship with ourselves right. If you are not able to understand yourself and what you are all about how on earth can you expect anyone else to understand you enough to have an acceptable relationship with you?

Few people spend enough quality time with themselves. Let me make this clear, I am not talking here about simply spending time by yourself. You must not mix up spending time on your own with having quality time with yourself.

Here are some ways in which you can get to know yourself better.

Spend quality time with yourself. Ok, I have said that a few times now so what do I mean by it? Let me put it this way. If you wanted to get to know me, Frank Shapiro, better, what would you do? That's right; you would spend time with me, talk with me, laugh and cry with me. You would ask questions and <u>really</u> listen to the answers. You would pay attention to my body language and my emotions and get to know my opinion on lots of important issues as well as the trivial ones. You would get to know my likes and dislikes and ask about my ambitions, goals and dreams. Before long you would probably know what I am thinking before I think it. The longer you spend with me and communicate with me, the more this will be true.

Do you see where I am going with this? All of the things you would need to do with me so that you get to know me are exactly what you need to do with yourself to get to know yourself. If you and I just spend snatched little pockets of time with each and didn't communicate, ask questions or share emotions with each other instead of spending quality time together then we would not learn anything about each other. And the same goes for the time you spend with yourself. By simply spending time on your own you will not learn much about yourself. You need to probe deeper, you need to talk with yourself and just as important you need to listen to yourself to understanding who you really are.

When your relationship with yourself improves then you will find that your relationships with other people also improve.

Relationship With Other Famous People.

The relationship that one famous person has with another can often be a tricky one as there are likely to be many other factors involved, such as competition and ego to name a few.

Having a career which is played out in the public eye means that you are, rightly or wrongly compared with other people like you. You are in an industry that often demands that you get to the top of the tree by being the best at what you do and beating other people who want the same thing. In actual fact this is no different from many other professions except that your competition is done in public. It doesn't matter if you are a famous athlete, politician, actor, writer or celebrity, getting to be number one is usually the aim and that means a public contest. Having managed some huge egos I am pretty sure that most people want to be number one in what they do, even if they don't openly admit it. I would imagine that most ultimately run the government. Similarly actors want their film to be the biggest box office of the year and to earn the most per picture. Athletes at all levels want to win; they want to come first which means they need to be ahead of the opposition.

Celebrity is about fame, and fame is about being on the front cover of magazines and there is only one front cover to each magazine so the more you are on it the less others will be.

The entertainment industry is a prime example where auditions are usually the way to get jobs. One hundred hopefuls are competing for one spot and only one person gets the gig. This is the way up and coming stars move up the ladder but this competition doesn't usually stop until you reach super star status and even then you may still need to read for a part. Competition does not stop when you have 'made it'. At this stage in your career it is more likely that if you are not considered for a part it's because someone else is flavour of the month or year.

So friendship with your peers can be very tricky unless you have clear boundaries on which the friendship can survive where both of you know where the line is drawn between what you have as friends and your careers. A true friendship between two people in the industry can usually only come about when you are not a threat to each other. The other way that friendship can work between two famous people is if you were solid friends before either of you achieved fame. Knowing that you can be yourself and trust the other person is vital for a strong bond, so for this to happen, you both need to know that the other will be your friend before fame, during fame and especially after celebrity fades.

Relationship with non-famous people.

Any relationship that you have with someone who does not share your notoriety again comes down to trust.

When I first began coaching people who were famous, one of the biggest hurdles I came up against was making sure that my client could trust me. I don't mean trust me as in trusting that I wouldn't steal their watch. No the trust that needs to exist is one that confirms to the person who is famous that the person who is not famous wants to be with them because of them and not because of their fame.

This is probably one of the biggest obstacles that any celebrity has to overcome.

Having spoken to many people in this situation, some of the questions that they ask themselves are; do these people want to know me because of my position or because we get on well? Can I trust the motives of this person for wanting to get close to me? Does this person have a hidden agenda for coming into my life?

You might think that this paranoia only applies to non-family but it is amazing how some long lost relatives suddenly come out the woodwork when your picture appears in their favourite glossy. Relatives who never made any attempt to be in your life before suddenly want to get close. These are the people who will quickly ignore or disown you when you are not such a big star.

This again all comes down to trust. Can you trust the person, family or not, to be a loyal friend and to want to be your friend just because of 'who' you are and not because of 'what' you are. Knowing, understanding and being confident within yourself are the key issues to overcoming this. Being suspicious of everyone new who comes into your life is not healthy so you need to have some kind of mechanism which will enable you to know who you can and who you cannot trust. Use your instincts and be suspicious of people who don't want to take the time to get to know you and want to be your instant best friend.

Successfully weeding out the people who are more interested in your fame than in you can be the key to how you deal with your fane. Save yourself a lot of pain and make your life a lot easier by knowing who to let into the inner sanctum of your life.

Relationship with your intimate partner.

Intimate relationships can fall into all or any of the above categories of relationships. Your intimate partner or potential intimate partner may be famous, non famous, someone you were friends with before you were famous or not.

One thing is for sure though; if the relationship is to work, you need two things to be in place. The first is mutual trust and the second is for you both to respect one another as individuals.

If the relationship you have with each other is based on anything other than an attraction to the core being, then the relationship is sure to falter and more often than not will happen sooner rather than later. If the attraction is based on the lifestyle you have, for example parties, red carpets and luxury travel then that person is connecting with your physical life and not your emotional one.

Communication is key to any successful relationship whether it is a public relationship or not. And don't only rely on verbal communication to stay close to each other. Pay attention to what goes on behind the talk. What do your actions towards each other tell you about your feelings for each other? How do you behave when you are alone, is it the same as when you are in public? What chemistry, sexual and non-sexual, do you have that is not based on your public image? Why is he/she attracted to you and you to him/her? Do you as a couple share the same beliefs, life values and goals? This doesn't mean you should give up your individual goals beliefs and values. It simply means remaining an individual with the understanding that you have a partner who must be considered for you both to move forward as a couple.

Build your relationship slowly and do not be lulled into the circus of a whirlwind romance. They rarely work even when the glare of the public is not on you. Try to get away from the limelight for a bit, even if it is only for a week or two so that you have the time to get to know each other without having paparazzi hounding you. Try to go somewhere that you are able to do normal things like eat in a restaurant or go to the cinema without being recognised. When you get back into public life, it is often a good idea to keep the relationship away from the media so that you can still enjoy some privacy for a while.

Give your relationship a chance by simply being yourselves from the start.

Gaining New Friends

This is a tricky issue for most people who find themselves in the grips of fame. The dilemma is, does this person want to be around me because of 'what' I am or because of 'who' I am?

It is difficult, but not impossible, for you, because of your high profile, to trust people who want to spend time with you. Many celebrities have had previous bad experiences of failed friendships and so are cautious that new people only want to be with them for the wrong reasons. After all, as a celebrity you are probably surrounded most of the time by people who gain in some way from you being who you are. And lets face it most of these people will probably disappear as soon as your fame, money or status starts to dwindle. So how do you trust the person who says they want to be your friend?

Trust in this context is based very much on attraction. I want to make it clear here that I am not talking about physical attraction. The attraction to which I refer is the spiritual attraction that makes you want to be around the other person and makes them want to be around you. For you to trust the other person whether he or she is famous or not, you need to spend time with them as mentioned earlier. For you to want to spend quality time with them you need to have mutual attraction; a bond that initiates a desire to be in each others company. By spending time with the person you will, if you have honed your own judgement skills, be able to decide whether this person is around for reasons that are different from genuine friendship.

Listen out for the tell tale signs that may help you decide if they as genuine as they make out.

Do they talk about your fame a lot?

Do they seem as happy and content when they are not around you as when they are?

Do they seem in awe of you and of the other celebrities?

Do they agree with everything you say or are they not afraid of disagreeing and having their own opinion?

Try not to be needy for friendship. In other words don't go looking for it. If you do the chances are that you will not find the genuine article but instead you will find 'fly by night' friends who are there in the good times and desert you in the bad.

Living life in the public glare can be a difficult and lonely place and the desire to have a close buddy can often drive you to hunt for a special friend. Genuine friends will find you most of the time. You will attract them by just being your true and authentic self. If you put on a false mask and pretend to be someone you really are not then you will attract false friends. If on the other hand you are genuine as a person, living the real 'who', then like minded people will come into your life and there will be a mutual attraction.

They are expected to own fast cars and a huge house or houses and to wear expensive clothes and jewellery. If they travel anything but first class around the world and stay in luxury hotels then their image would suffer and their standing in the world of celebrity be diminished.

It is important to listen and take advice from trusted financial advisors on all financial situations. But the most sensible and down to earth advice anyone should be giving you is to live within your means no matter how wealthy or famous you are, so that you can continue to enjoy the rewards of your success even after your earning power goes.

Boredom

How can someone who is rich, famous and who has hoards of people around them be bored I hear you ask? One possible answer is that when a person reaches a certain status in the fame game they don't need to work as much as they do when they are struggling for success.

Boredom can be overcome by making sure that what you are doing in your career and private life is what you are truly interested in.

Take for example the way in which some musicians may think. They may see a great opportunity to have the life that they want to have and make a lot of money by achieving success through being a 'pop' artist. This may not actually be the type of music that they are passionate about and so will get very bored with it once they reach a certain standard of success with it.

Invest money wisely

I will talk about money in more detail later in the book as this is a big one for everyone not only the rich and/or famous.

I am not a financial advisor and what I say here is not meant as advice. I am simply making some observations about money which to me seem like basic common sense.

I am a great believer that the only way to invest for the future financially is to make sure that no matter how much or little you earn you must invest proportionately. In other words if you earn little then invest little but when you earn more make sure you invest the same percentage as before.

The popular theory is that no matter how little you make, you can never start to build your savings and investments too soon.

The problem is that when you are famous everyone expects you also to be wealthy. Although this is often the case it is not always true. Many celebrities, especially songwriters, earn money from royalties and although the income is pretty much guaranteed, can take months or years to reach you. Performers and writers may receive an advance on royalties and this will mean that they will be paying the money back long after they get it. So planning is vital especially in such an unpredictable business.

The other problem is that when you reach a higher status you may feel that you have a certain image to maintain. This can create a real challenge for some celebrities as they feel obliged to maintain the image their public expects from them.

I have known of many musicians who made a success out of doing something which they would rather not be doing. Yes, they want to be making music but not the kind of music that will bring the success they are looking for. The problem arises when, after attaining a certain level of success churning out the kind of music that will sell but that they do not enjoy playing, they try their hand at the music they do enjoy.

One thing that I have learned in just about any business I have been involved in is not to change a winning formula. Yet many musicians and actors do this very thing. An actor who finds success in a television sitcom series may feel that he or she wants to stretch their acting ability by doing some serious stage work only to find that they are not making the success of it that they did before and find that paying for the lifestyle to which they have become accustomed is impossible.

Musicians who have one or two hit albums playing commercial music which is not really their passion, often find that the next album they release, which is full of music they do like, flops.

After all most people in the entertainment industry are creative people and as such they will probably at some stage in their career feel the need to experiment with the music or acting that they really like which often has adverse effect on their success.

You can also find that you get yourself into a similar situation in your private life.

Take for example a person who is not a natural party animal but who goes to every party and event they can just for the exposure and to get publicity. They will almost certainly find that they get very bored with this type of living very quickly.

The thing to remember if you want to really overcome boredom in your life is to live life as an individual and do the things that are in line with your real self. It is a pointless exercise to pretend to be who you are not. If it is not in line with who you are then it will be short lived. If you are reading this and are enjoying success as a celebrity you must continue to do the things in life as if you were as anonymous as everyone else.

Look at your true values and discover your what you are truly passionate about. It is not as easy to know what floats your boat as it sounds. Try looking at the small things in life that, when you do them, make time pass really quickly. Pursue hobbies and activities with friends you have who are not living their life in the limelight.

Stay grounded by remaining as 'normal' as possible so that you are living in the real world as your authentic self and not the fantasy world which is created only by the circumstance of your celebrity status.

Loneliness

Throughout my time as a life coach I have come across many people who speak of aloneness as a negative. Even though, as a someone who lives the celebrity lifestyle which includes having people around you most of the time, the feeling of loneliness can be strong and lead to a whole lot of negativities in your life.

If this applies to you and you can relate to this then ask yourself if it is possible for you to turn that negative feeling of loneliness round so that you think of occasional aloneness as a positive thing. How do I do that I hear you ask. Well, if you are able to start to appreciate the alone time you have by looking at it as a situation which allows you the time and space to just 'be' yourself, then you are on your way to making this time more productive and less of a negative in your life.

Rediscover what the great things are that you can do when you are totally on your own? What are you able to do when there are no other people around that you cannot do when they are there? How can you use the time you spend on your own in a way that will fulfil a need or a want that normal life cannot give you?

Remember that there is a huge difference between aloneness i.e. being alone, and being lonely. Being alone is physical, while being lonely is emotional. It has nothing to do with how many people are around you and is more to do with how much of a spiritual connection you have with people whether they are physically with you or not.

But before you can start to feel true connections with

anyone else you need to find the true connection you have with yourself. By spending the alone time productively you will strengthen this connection with yourself and so help you connect with others.

Being lonely often comes from a lack of connection with others. What happens when you are feeling this, is that you are mixing up the idea that you can only connect with people who are physically with you.

That is not quite true. Amazingly we are all able to "connect with" people who are not actually with us physically. If you think about it, there are people, both present and past with whom you have a connection; loved ones who have passed on or close family or friends who have moved to live in a different part of the world. It is this connection with them, even though they are not physically with you that stops you from being lonely.

I suggest that loneliness does not happen because you are alone, it happens because there is no one in your immediate physical environment with whom you feel a connection.

So why not break the two apart until they naturally come together for you. Stop the feeling of loneliness by connecting to your soul mates around the world and enjoy the physical company of the people you are around right now without trying to connect with them. The connection with those physically around you will come through time without either of you trying.

The ultimate, of course, is when you are physically with someone with whom you also connect. This does happen but cannot be rushed. It will happen in its own time, and probably when you least expect it.

Over indulgence

This is an area that most of us will be able to understand as most of us find it easy to overindulge in certain parts of our lives at some time during our life.

For someone who has a limited personal life, few activities and lots of spare cash, it is the easiest thing in the world to overindulge. Both boredom and a hectic lifestyle can be key factors as to why people who live their life in the limelight overindulge. The main ways in which this shows itself can be an indulgence in food, drugs, drink, sex or misuse of their body in some other way.

This is much simpler to control if avoided completely from the outset or is nipped in the bud as soon as it starts. Being aware that overindulgence can be a potential problem can be a useful tool in making sure it never gets a hold on you.

This is all about understanding your short term and long term objectives and keeping focussed on what you really want to achieve from life. I am sure that when you were at the early phase of thinking about being famous, people would ask why you wanted to be famous. Your reply may have sounded something like; well I want enough money to live life to the full or I am doing it for the glamour the status the recognition etc. I am equally sure you did not mention … oh and I would like to overindulge in drugs or in self abuse.

Keeping yourself focussed and having the ability to be able to keep your feet firmly on the ground will go a long way to helping you not overindulge.

If however you find that you are displaying signs of

overindulgence of any substance, be it food, drugs or alcohol then seek help in ways in which you can stop it before it takes hold and starts to control your life. This is not only true of substances but is equally valid for overindulgence in activities. An addiction to a certain lifestyle or sex for example can be equally as damaging to your career and your personal life.

Seek help from people you can trust and if you find it is getting too much for you then seek out a reputable professional.

Ego

Question: What is it about people in the limelight that makes them so egotistical?

Answer: Those around them.

When a person is famous for whatever reason, they are almost always surrounded by 'yes men' and 'yes women'.

Who or what are yes men and women? These are people who are only associating themselves with you because they make money out of what you do and who you are. For the most these people are not going to tell you that you are not good at what you do or should be doing things differently. They will continue, no matter what, to tell you how wonderful you are, to your face at least.

Being surrounded by these people will have an effect on how you perceive yourself and how you think about yourself. You will, at some stage, begin to believe the hype they create about you. Just as, when people repeatedly tell you how bad a person you are, and you take this to heart and start to believe them, when you surround yourself with people who constantly tell you how wonderful you are, then that sets your belief system going in that direction too.

Now don't get me wrong. Having positive people around you is a must as far as I am concerned. the more the better, but as well as being positive they must also be honest and true to themselves as well as true to you.

Surround yourself with positive well-balanced

individuals who have nothing at all to gain from hanging out with you or by telling it the way it is. Of course, you need positive people around you but caring, truthful people are the way to control your ego.

However, we can't just blame other people for any over inflated ego you may suffer from. You will develop this very well for yourself even without the help of others. After all if you are setting your sights on a career which will see you live out your life in public then you need to be ultra confident in yourself to be successful at the job you have. The key thing to remember if you do not want your ego to outgrow you is that you must be confident without being arrogant. The difference between confidence and arrogance is that confidence is internal, it comes from within and arrogance is external, it has external influences.

Being confidant is about doing whatever you do for you. You do things because you want to do the best you can and to the limit of your own capabilities. You do things because it brings you pleasure and is rewarding for reasons that are personal to you.

Being arrogant on the other hand is about doing whatever you do for other people. You do things to prove to others that you can do them. it may be that you are seeking approval of parents or that you have to show someone that you can actually achieve something with your life when they told you that you were unable to. Many teachers of young people are very much to blame for the negative way in which some of the young people in their care grow up.

Do what you do because you want it for yourself. By

doing this you will gain the appreciation and genuine admiration for the people who live you for who you are and who are around you for the right reasons.

By displaying arrogant behaviour, you will attract only those people who are in your company for unhealthy reasons and will do just about anything to make sure that they are getting what they need from associating themselves with you. These are the people who disappear from your life as soon as your fame fades.

Stage Three

After Fame

Before During **After**

Stage 3 - After Fame

I once saw an interview in which the actor Richard Dreyfuss spoke of his life, his successes and his regrets. He said something along the lines of; life somehow seemed more exciting and fulfilling while I was pursuing success than it is now that I have achieved it.

This is a powerful statement for an actor who is amongst the top in his field. But this feeling is true for many people and because I have coached quite a few people in the entertainment industry, I have heard many stories from others with similar feelings of being unfulfilled even though they seem to have success.

Dreyfuss also intimated that life, although seen as a success by many people, did not hold the same magic as he thought it might especially after achieving a hard fought for goal.

Richard Dreyfuss obviously knew very early on in his life that he wanted to be an actor. This was his dream, his passion and his focus. His drive may have been that he wanted to have all the trappings that being rich and famous would bring; to be recognised in the street, be able to afford things he felt important in life and to hear people say; "there goes Richard Dreyfuss". His road to fame was apparently long and hard. He told the interviewer of how he went for audition after audition with most ending in the casting director shouting 'NEXT'. He, like many wannabe actors had little money and low self- esteem because of all the rejections he suffered in these early days but his focus was fixed on what he considered to be the end result; fame. Yet once he got what he wanted, once he actually achieved his goal, he discovered that looking forward to being famous was in some strange way more satisfying than actually being famous. Having the goal was the very thing that inspired and motivated him and he possibly saw no further than that one particular dream.

Many actors from all corners of the world feel this way because of the nature of the career they have chosen, but isn't it true that many people, actors or not, feel the same way after they achieve a big goal?

It is as if looking to the future is more fulfilling than living in the present.

For many people looking forward to a vacation can often be more exciting than the vacation itself. The anticipation of the end result drives us on but when it is reached there is a feeling of discontent.

Why should this be so? It may be that the dream or goal was not as rewarding as you expected it to be, or that it is just as you imagined it would be or even better, but we are too busy looking for the next dream to enjoy the results of this one. It may even simply be that you have no next goal and the feeling of "I have arrived" is not as sweet as you expected.

Success is ongoing. Life is the goal we must focus on with all the other little goals being the stepping stones to success. If we think about life in this way then it is easy to understand that it is a continuous journey with no defining end result. It may be helpful to think of reaching goals as stepping-stones along the road to success. When a train arrives at its final destination it sits in the station and waits. It has nowhere else to go. On its journey to its final destination however, it has tasks or goals to achieve. It must stop at each station with its engine running, paused in readiness to move forward.

Success will never be fully achieved until each of us takes our final breath. The secret is to enjoy the journey and grasp the magnificence of each day. Enjoy the present no matter where you are on your personal journey. Whether you are working hard at achieving one of your goals or paused, heading for the next one, live fully in the present moment but remember to enjoy the journey.

.

Rejection

The initial shock of having no job offers and having nothing but bills drop though your letter box can be a devastating reality and can be blamed on many things. But when push comes to shove there is not a lot you can do about it when the media, the public or your fans have decided you are not the big news you once were.

Coming to terms with rejection in an industry where being knocked back is more common than in most other professions, is not easy. Dealing with rejection takes inner strength. No one wants to think of themselves as not being wanted but if you base the journey you travel on life and not on fame then nothing actually has stopped.

The scenery of your life has changed but in actual fact if you look at yourself closely then you will discover that you are the same person you always were. In fact you are the same person throughout your journey; before you were famous, during your fame period and now, after your fame has gone.

Living life as yourself throughout each stage can and will help you deal with the unavoidable feeling of rejection after your fame goes. It will help you maintain personal goals far beyond the glitz of celebrity. Design your life so that you are not living in your past glory or trying to recreate the good old days. Today is the present and it is how it is. Now it is your job to create this day, this week, month or year the way you want it to be. Do not start thinking about this stage of your life when it is upon you, by then it is far too late. You must be planning for and anticipating this stage during the height of your success. It is inevitable that it will come unless you are unfortunately taken from this earth prematurely while still at your peak. This stage of your career should not come as any great surprise because just as we all know that our life will come to an end at some stage in the future, famous people should realise that at some point their fame is going to wane.

Plan for it and move forward. Whether it is a comeback you plan for or life as a mere mortal, make sure you do it in a way that keeps you strong within yourself.

You are still You

You are still 'who' you are even though you might not feel you are 'what' you used to be.

That sounds a bit complicated, so let me say it in a slightly different way. What you are may change several times throughout your life, but who you are will remain constant. This again has a lot to do with forward planning.

Planning for your career, from the day you set out to be a star to the day you will fall will pay dividends in the long run. This sounds a bit negative and inflexible but in actual fact it is the reality of your situation and one of the ways that you can deal with the eventual decline which the great majority of people in the fame game go through. No one can take your identity away from you except you and this is why it is vital that you live your life as a down to earth individual even when you live your life in the public eye. Staying grounded and having the people who are your true friends around you will usually ensure that you come through the whole of your career in good shape.

Things that you should expect to happen to you in the twilight of your career will include some of the following:

Loss of status

What happened to my favourite table in the restaurant?

What do you mean I can't get bumped up to first class?

Why is the suite taken by someone else in the hotel?

Loss of entourage

What happened to my friends? Were they really friends? Not if they desert you at the same time as your fame.

Where did my security people go?

Where is my driver?

Where is my publicist?

Loss of finances

Financial advisors seem a little less interested.

Did you spend spend spend or did you invest wisely for the inevitable?

Should I get the car that is second top of the range?

Are the loss of status, entourage and finances enough to make you want to try for a comeback? Can you, and do you want, to reinvent yourself and try to do it all again? Are you still as focussed as you used to be? Do you still have your fans? Do you still have the hunger? Do you still have the talent?

The loss of all the perks that come along with the lifestyle that you have become accustomed to can be a painful experience and one that can drive individuals who should know better to try and rebuild what should be left alone.

Before you dive back in and try for a comeback, take a

while to think about what you are doing or at least trying to do. Most comebacks fail because the fans have moved on. If they hadn't moved on then you would still be at the height of your success and you would not need to attempt to make a comeback.

Ask yourself if you need the money or if you are content with what you have and try to work out why it is that you want to put yourself through all that again. Your fans have memories, and it is best to leave them with great memories of you rather than of the person who needed to prove themselves by making a comeback but failed.

And Finally

Whether you are striving for fame, at the height of your celebrity or at the stage where nobody remembers who you used to be, the one thing that will allow you to move forward is that each morning you waken you have choice. You have the choice to let others decide what the day is going to be like for you or for you to make that decision for yourself.

You, after all are you. You are in control of your own life's outcome. No one else knows you better than you do and you have the opportunity every single day to make that day the beginning of the rest of your life. While it is a cliché to say that today is the beginning of the rest of your life, it is in actual fact true. Sitting around thinking of what could be or might have been or what once was won't make your future dreams come true. You on the other hand can make your dreams a reality by remembering that no matter what stage in life or of your career you are at, it is simply just a stage in your life. And what is your life? Yes, that's right it is a journey, so go out there and enjoy it.

Why The Famous Fear Fame

Fame Increases POWER, it can decrease the sense of CONTROL, which often increases STRESS.

Problems and challenges may arise for someone who is famous because of things they do to themselves like taking drugs, abusing drink or indulging in some other kind of abnormal behaviour. They may also arise because of external influences like people taking advantage of them or capitalising on their insecurities and fame. It doesn't really matter how they come to find themselves facing challenges, the reality is the same whenever this happens; he or she gives control to something else or someone else.

It is only when they realise that what they are doing should not be under the control of other people, that they can begin to do something about it and instead be totally in control of their own destiny. It is of no relevance if the problem is self-inflicted, has occurred because of the actions of other people or because of any other reason. It is vital to understand the situation is all controllable by you. It doesn't matter who is trying to do what to you or what motives they have for doing it, it only matters what you decide to do with the knowledge that this is actually happening to you.

Most of us can and will react in a host of different ways to circumstances and pressure. To be honest no one knows how they would react to anything including the pressures that fame can bring, until it actually happens to them but one thing is for sure, every one of us is an individual human being and as such we all have choices. We all have the choice to take drugs, abuse alcohol, be moody or be happy and fulfilled. We all have the ability to say no before some of these things take hold and simply put, we all have the choice to be in total control of our life or not.

It is important to understand here that being in control of your own life is nothing to do with being controlling. You can be in control of your own life without trying to control any one else's life. When we put our own standards and expectations on to other people and try to manipulate and control them, our life starts to get out of control.

This is what happens when we feel the pressures of fame. We feel that other people and external situations are beginning to, or at least attempting to control and manipulate us. This is when we fight back by rebelling and saying, 'this is not going to happen to me'. We think we can take control of our own life by doing things to ourselves and reacting in a way that only feeds the control that others have over us. Taking drugs, overusing alcohol or self-damaging the body are all examples of how we falsely think we can regain control. We try to regain our independence and individuality by being excessive in some way. This only serves to harm us.

The celebrities who take real control of their life or remain in control of their life are the ones who don't care what the outside world thinks or does and so aren't tempted into trying these things.

Their future vision for themselves is so powerful that their self image is strong no matter what. If they are confidant about themselves and about who they really are inside, and are confident of their own ability, they will remain grounded in reality instead of in fantasy. There is a huge difference between being confident and being aggressive, but many people mix these two things up. Often someone trying to be an individual will implode and become aggressive. They will not necessarily show this aggression in a physical way but in a rebellious way, falsely believing that by acting in this manner they will show the outside world their individuality. They will build barriers against anything that tries to invade the fantasy world they have created.

Confidence comes from within. It is internal. Aggression on the other hand is external. Confidence comes from not worrying about failure while aggression is based in failure and fear.

Aggression is displayed when we feel we have to prove ourselves to other people or to the rest of the world. Confidence on the other hand is much more about proving to yourself and living your life in the knowledge that you are doing exactly what it is you, as your own person, wants to do. It is not about the pressure and fear of being controlled by other people.

You see, at the inception of your dream to be famous there was probably no one there to tell you what to do. The core dream you had came from the desire to do what, as an ordinary non-famous person, you wanted to do. All of us, with a few exceptions like royal families of the world, were born not famous. Most of us were born as private individuals. And most of us were born with the inbuilt desire to make something of our selves and our lives. The dream and aspiration may have been to have a stable family life, to work in an office, be a surgeon or even to become famous. At the beginning of the desire to be famous there was no pressure from anyone else.

There was no pressure to be famous from anyone else and the aspiration to be that way was one of pure desire, not one of fear. This desire is like an extension of your personality at that early stage. You start off being this individual with core values and beliefs and gradually add the desire to be a famous actor, singer, performer or politician, or just to be famous.

Those with that burning desire to capture the limelight feel the need to add to who they already are. There comes a point though, often when you start to be recognised in the street, that the desire shifts from being internal (because you really want it for yourself), to being external which is driven from the outside influences of the people who want you to be the person they think you are. You may, at this point find yourself being driven by fear instead of desire. This is often when the difficulties and challenges can begin. When you cross the line from doing things because you want to, to doing them because other people want you to, then trouble is not far away.

At this point you may find yourself being motivated to carry on because of the fear of letting other people down, rather than the joy that doing what you do brings you. Even if your desire is to carry on with your career and reach new heights, it can often be difficult to be motivated from within in your attempt to move forward instead of being motivated by the fear of not succeeding.

[1]Ruby Wax is reported to regard herself as work in

progress and has often talked about celebrity as being a hindrance to self growth. Like many well-known people she enjoys the perks which fame often brings, like upgrades on flights to first class or the best table at a restaurant. But she maintains that fame can seriously damage your health. Ruby has, I am sure met many hundreds of celebrities, not only on a personal level but also for her various documentary series on celebrities and is confident that being at ease with fame is the exception to the rule with paranoia and insecurity being the norm.

[2]Hugh Grant put it in a nutshell when he said that he feels exhausted from it all and confesses that while he is not unhappy with his lifestyle he does feel that he has too much career and too little home life. Some of his not so famous friends apparently envy his seemingly happy-go-lucky bachelor lifestyle while others see his life as a less than blissful existence, and as a man with so much wealth and success who still goes home to an empty house.

Wealth, success and superficial happiness without a deep feeling of self-fulfilment can be an empty and lonely place. Even with a few close friends, hundreds of acquaintances and millions of adoring fans, the life of a celebrity can be a lonely and isolated existence.

What came first, the chicken or the egg? It's a well-known conundrum with a few serious implications. Here is another one for you to ponder as you sip your cocoa of an

---

[1] Mail on Sunday Magazine YOU 29th June 2003

[2] Daily Mail 23rd June 2003

evening; are those who reach the dizzy heights of fame insecure because they are famous or are they famous because they are insecure?

As young children we often acted out scenes of fantasy. We put on our parents most stylish cloths and pretended to be adults. We floated around in high heeled shoes that were five times too big for us, dresses that trailed around behind and put on makeup so thick that we might have been mistaken for clowns. And that was just the boys! We would spend hours playing doctors and nurses or cowboys and indians or indulge in some other pastime that would allow us to act out roles that were nothing more than an escape from reality.

As kids we can get away with escaping from reality. In fact as kids we can get away with almost anything. As adults however to escape the realism of everyday life in the pursuit of something dreamlike, we either need to be mad or hope to end up in a career where life is just one big fantasy: acting.

The aim of most people as they begin their chosen career is to be the best. If you go into medicine you hope to reach the top of your profession and be the best doctor in the world. Similarly, you embark on a career in retail you hope to be the biggest most profitable retailer in the land. Being the best at what you do, as with most other things in life can be achieved with little worry about the consequences. Acting however is different.

To be the best actor means that you will, by the very nature of the job, be famous. Being famous, although exciting at first, can wear on the nerves a bit and more importantly cannot be undone. People who achieve fame cannot retire and return to obscurity when it is all over even if the decision to retire is made by others. They can hide in the hills and never come out of the front door, but they cannot re-enter 'normality' as an unknown.

What is it that drives anyone into a business that has no ending? Many people who seek out fame as a way of life were exceptional at the dressing up games as children. They excelled in the art of fantasy. In fact, they were so good at pretending to be someone else that it may have almost become easier to live in fantasy than to live a life of insecurity like many ordinary people do.

The question for us mere unknown mortals to ponder is not why the famous become so paranoid and insecure, but why so many insecure people rise up as magnificent superstars. But this is nothing more than a vicious circle because this then adds to the inbuilt insecurity of who they really are.

Insecurity brings us back to lack of control and lack of control can lead those most vulnerable to losing themselves in self abuse.

Let's face it. living the life of super stardom has many advantages; luxury lifestyle, excessive wealth, homes in far off lands and, well, just about anything they want. And it is that last part that really can drive them into deeper and deeper insecurity. They just about have it all, but they can never have what many of them discover is the most precious thing of all which money can't buy, privacy. Insecurity breeds fear of just about anything and anybody. Real friends disappear and in their place appear new sycophantic ones. Often the stress of feeling trapped in a bubble of fame and not being able to pop in and out of the childlike fantasy world they once enjoyed, makes the famous feel less in control of their own destiny.

But not all who find fame encounter a life which is hard to deal with. There are many examples of very well-adjusted individuals who manage to have a hugely successful public life while retaining an equally successful private life.

What then is the difference? Why is it that some who reach the top in acting seem to implode and be unable to handle it while others handle it just like another day at the office?

Attitude is the answer. You see, children know when the fantasy of dressing up stops and reality starts. They know that, as they play in the garden at cowboys and indians and are made to come in because it is time to for lunch or to get a bath and go to bed, the fantasy stops and reality returns. Many of the famous have got so used to living the fantasy that it is almost impossible to separate it from the reality.

Children while being allowed to explore their creative fantasies are kept grounded by reality because their parents have the power of authority. In the case of the famous, they themselves have the power because the only other people in their lives are people who would not contradict them. They are mainly surrounded by 'yes men' and 'yes women' who dare not suggest that they return to reality let alone that reality even exists. Why would they? It is surely not in their interest to have their famous paymaster be an 'ordinary' person.

So, look out ordinary person who wants to be famous. It's not all bad by any manner of means, but if you seek fame without realising that you are entering a life of fantasy, which must be based in the reality of the person you really are, the

insecurity that pushed you forward to achieve your dream
might just be the very thing that creates your downfall.

Respect – Power - Money
The key to being a Top Celebrity

***Respect**, you cannot gain without power.*
***Power**, you cannot gain without money.*
***Money** is found through vision, passion and focus*
(Unknown)

The world of celebrity is not always run by the same rules as the outside world. In the world of the rich and famous money talks and power is everything. Only when you have these things, then might you gain respect. This however is not the case in non celebrity land. Respect can be and often is earned by people who genuinely deserve it. Mother Teresa was not a wealthy woman but commanded great respect and she certainly wielded power when it came to world leaders as they sat up and took notice of what she had to say.

But we must also remember that respect is three-fold; it is internal in the form of respect one has for oneself, self respect, it is external in the form of the respect you have for others and for the world, and it also is about the respect other people have for you.

Respect for oneself is one thing but to be respected by other people is an entirely different thing. Each of us can choose to have a high opinion of ourselves or not, but we cannot make others automatically feel the same way about us. Respect from others is earned. It is earned in different ways depending on whether you have celebrity status or not, but earned all the same.

No matter how much money we have, we simply cannot buy the respect of other people, although often we are able to buy their attention and even their apparent friendship. However, money although not the be all and end all, is an important part of the equation of being respected.

Being confident enough to take the long-term view in a profession where others only look for instant success is a brave thing. There are people out there who would do just about anything to achieve short term fame. Taking the long-term challenge is real power.

Money can buy you power which can often gain you respect. It is a strange thing but even the nastiest of people who have enough money, which in turn brings them power, can very often gain respect.

Take as an example of how this can work some senior USA politicians. Now I want to make it clear that I am not implying that any of them are nasty. Do you imagine that many of the previous Presidents would have been so widely respected for the views they held if they had not had the money to gain them the power of entering into office? Yes they would have had the same views on important things as an unknown, but it is only when they could find enough money to get themselves heard on a national level, that they suddenly became powerful enough to run for the presidency. Then if things went well for them during their term they end up being respected for their views, which were the same as before they had the power, except without the respect.

So the statement that money can buy power is a true statement which is a reality in a world where fantasy runs riot.

But what most people don't realise is that you don't need to have money to start the process. Another statement that is equally true is 'Apparent money can buy you apparent power which gains you respect'. One does not in fact need either money or power to actually gain respect from others. All that is needed is for others to perceive that you have these things.

Take for example the man who saves up all year and hires a top of the range convertible Bentley sports car for a day, who can give the appearance (for that one day) of having money. In doing so he gives the appearance of having wealth, which in turn gains a certain amount of respect from people who see him driving it. It is not the car itself which brings respect but the hard work and dedication to business that must have been needed to bring the money to buy such an object which is respected.

But driving such a toy is not enough to gain lasting respect. If it were known that he had merely hired the car for the day or even that it is in fact father's little toy, which the chameleon has sneakily taken for a spin, then any respect that anyone had for him will almost certainly disappear. To gain real lasting respect, as well as having the car in his possession, he also needs add to the illusion and maintain the charade. Pulling up in front of a top restaurant in full view of the fellow diners needs to be followed up with a confident statement such as "I don't have a table but I would like to dine here tonight". Waiting in line for a table would simply give his game away.

Spending money is easy, or so it would seem. Did you ever see the movie Brewster's Millions? This was a movie where the character played by Richard Prior inherited millions of dollars. The only problem was that his long lost relative had given him a task to complete before the poor man could inherit anything. The task was to spend 3 million dollars within a set period of time. He couldn't tell anyone why he was spending the money nor could he give more than a small percentage of it to charity. To make it even more difficult his benefactor made it clear that he could not be left with any assets at the end of his spending spree. He simply had to spend it. Suffice to say Prior found himself in some hilarious situations trying to spend the money.

To spend money with meaning and style takes a certain type of person. As a celebrity it may be that you have come into money rather quickly. Having been paid next to nothing as a struggling performer, songwriter or actor you may strike it lucky and suddenly finding a mega recording contract being offered to you or a financial number with a few more zeros at the end of it being transferred into your account for a part in a blockbuster movie. All this can be challenging to someone if they are not used to handling the vast amounts of money which the modern superstars find themselves with.

Choosing how to spend your money should always be a thoughtful process. Remember back to when you had none and you chose carefully how to spend what you had. Now that you have money the process should be similar even though you are dealing in larger amounts. That car you bought when you were financially challenged was a fourth-hand banger but you saved for it then worked out the best way to spend your hard earned cash on the car of your choice. The same process still applies when you have money except the car you buy is brand new and a bit larger.

How you spend your money says a lot about you. Spend it without thought and you will appear to other people as unthoughtful or even brash. Spend it too carefully and you will come across as mean and ill spirited. There is a balance. No one will judge you for having the best of things when you can afford it but how you acquire the best of things is how you will be judged.

So where should you spend your money now that you know how to spend it? Well, there are the myriad of clubs around the world all eager to welcome you. Remember that certain clubs are the right places to be seen spending money and others are completely wrong if you want to keep your image intact. The same goes for restaurants. Fine dining comes at a price and although you do not need a menu with the cost of the food on it, knowing the price of things shows that you care about money which in turn shows that you care about yourself and others.

Remember also that exclusivity costs money. There are many places as a star that you will gain access to that you did not even know existed as a mere nobody. Doors will open without you needing to push them. In fact the strange thing about this phenomenon is that in many places you are treated to free things. It is a bit of a sign of the whole celebrity concept that when you are poor and need free things like clothes and bling, you need to pay for them yourself but as you rise to superstardom people either give you free things to wear or even better, pay you to wear them.

Yes it is a strange old world indeed.

By now you may be starting to realise that the respect others have for you and the money you have can bring you a certain amount of power.

To be Famous you must be an entrepreneur

One of the most important things to realise about being famous is that you will also need to be an entrepreneur.

Having good entrepreneurial skills will help you promote yourself in creative and exciting ways. Without the drive and determination that all great entrepreneurs have, the chances of you reaching the top will be greatly reduced. If you do get there and have not honed some entrepreneurial skills then you will probably not be able to maintain your position.

There are hundreds of millions of people in the world but if I had to ask you to name 100 famous people you would probably struggle. Try it, it sounds easier than you think. The same is true for great entrepreneurs. There are lots of business people in the world but you might struggle to name a handful of well-known successful ones.

So, for you to be famous you need to be one of the very few who beat the odds and get to be one of the few that are remembered.

Notice that most successful celebrities are also very shrewd business people. Almost all at some time or other start their own business, usually built round their own brand, which is of course themselves. They set up their own clothing, perfume or other product and sell them under their own name. Even when they are involved in charity work they are using their entrepreneurial skills to sell themselves in a way that benefits the charity to which they give their support.

Paris Hilton has a string of successful product lines. Paul Newman has a very successful food business from which he donates the profits to charity. Most celebrities who have these creative entrepreneurial skills, have brand appeal and bring out all sorts of products bearing their name and image.

It is true to say that many of them make as much money from this side of their life as they do from being the celebrity that people know them for.

What is it that you need to know or need to do to be a successful entrepreneur?

First of all, you need to know what it is that you want to achieve. If you don't set goals for yourself then how on earth will you know when you get there? Set your long-term goal and then to make it easier for you to achieve, break it into manageable small ones.

The next thing that you should look into is getting a mentor. The best way to achieve what you want is to find someone who has already done it. It sounds simple but few people do it. Successful people love to mentor up-and-coming prodigies. Do your homework and find someone who has already done what you want to do and ask them to be your mentor.

Think about hiring a Life Coach. Sorry, but I couldn't resist the blatant plug. With the right coach on your side, you will have someone with you every step of the way, giving you unconditional support and helping you take the necessary action needed to have your goals come to fruition.

The next thing you must make sure you do is to equip yourself with the right tools to do the job. The tools of your job, if you want to be a singer, is a great vocal coach, an actor will have an acting coach and so on. But don't just equip yourself with the basics. Find yourself a stylist who will make sure that you are seen in clothes that will give the right impression to those who see you and help you to have the right attitude towards yourself. All the tools you will need are out there so go get them and use them.

The next thing you must do is less physical and more emotional. Self belief is like having a hidden weapon. It is similar to when your favourite sporting team plays a game in front of their home crowd. They feel the support and so have the advantage. Never doubt yourself or that you will make it to where you want to go. Most people who are determined to be the best they can be either in business or in the entertainment industry rarely doubt themselves. We all have times when a little demon sits on our shoulder and reminds us that we are only human and that humans often fail. These are the times when we need to hold on to the belief that we can and will make it and that we will do whatever it takes to achieve all we want.

Next you must surround yourself with people who have the same or similar vision as you. If you are an entrepreneur or business person then you want to hang about with other entrepreneurs and business people. They will have a similar mindset to you and will tend to think in the same way as you. They will often have the same confidence and goals as you have. You will learn from them just as they will learn from you and when things go well you can share your experiences with each other. On the other hand, when things are going not so well, then you will find comfort and encouragement by being with people who know what you are going through. You don't see zebras hanging out with lions, do you? No, they hang around with other zebras so that they can all look out for each other and can learn how to feed and defend themselves from each other.

You must also stay focussed on your goals. Write your goals down; do not just try to remember them in your head. Your memory will get too cluttered, and some important goals will inevitably get lost. Remind yourself regularly what your most important goal is and why you want to achieve it. If your goal is to be wealthy then find a picture of your ideal home that you will only be able to afford when you have enough money to buy it. Pin it up somewhere so that you can remind yourself why you must remain focused even when things are not going as they should. Focus is the key to success in anything that you do and is a skill that will stand you in good stead for the future.

In my capacity as a public speaker, I am often asked to give special interest talks to passengers on cruise ships. On one such trip I was taking my usual 7am stroll round the promenade deck when I saw two of the crew having a heated discussion about how to complete the task they had been given to do, which was to wash the huge array of windows around the ship.

One was convinced the best way to do this was to wash them slowly, take his time and keep his head down and out of trouble. By taking a long time to do the job he surmised that he would not be asked to do anything else once his task was done. The other had a different theory. He wanted to work fast and finish the windows quickly. I imagined that this was possibly because he would then be able to skive and sit with his feet up for a few hours before returning to his boss for another task.

How wrong I was. When I asked him his reason he told me that he wanted to do this job well and efficiently because the sooner he completed the window washing the sooner he could go back to his boss and ask for more work. Confused, I asked why this was to his advantage as he was not on bonus for the number of tasks done in a day. He replied that he had a plan, a long-term plan. By being efficient and making sure that his boss recognised his efficiency he would be noticed by those up the chain of command. Getting noticed for his good work and enthusiasm would eventually get him promotion. Getting promotion would mean that he would be the one telling others, like his slow friend, what tasks to do. "No more window washing for me" he said with a grin!

Another important part to this is to make sure that you reward yourself. No matter if the reward is a quiet evening listening to your favourite music while sipping a glass of wine or an extravagant new purchase; you must always reward yourself for your achievements. That is one of they the ways humans are programmed. We need to feel of value to others and especially to ourselves. The way to value yourself is to reward yourself for things well done. Each time you achieve a step forward towards your goal treat yourself to something no matter how small. This doesn't need to be a physical treat like a gift, although it can be, it can just as easily be a quiet dinner for you and your partner, a long walk along the beach or a few hours of 'me' time.

Know Your 'A's From Your 'B's

If 'Z' is to be unknown, then 'A' is to be known throughout the world. In reality you don't really need to go anywhere close to 'Z' to be an unknown. You only need go as far as 'D'.

What am I on about I hear you ask. There are imaginary lists in the celebrity land. Being on 'A' list will open the door to just about anywhere in the world. Shops will close to give you some personal shopping time, clubs will stay open for you and queuing is a thing of the past. In the wonderfully often unreal world of celebrity the difference between a true star; an 'A' lister and a wannabe, a 'B' lister, is very small. Just as the difference between a superstar and a has-been.

There are a few subtle and some not so subtle ways in with you can distinguish between an 'A' lister and a 'B' lister.

Here are some of them.

'A' listers look for a table in a restaurant where they will not be seen nor disturbed by the press or public. 'B' listers do all they can to get a table in a prominent position hoping people notice them and pay them some attention.

'A' listers use chauffeurs and have limos with darkened windows. 'B' listers hail cabs and roll the windows down so that people can see them.

'A' listers have shops close for them so they can do some private shopping. 'B' listers will be asked to attend the opening of new shops to cut the ribbon.

‘A’ listers complain quietly so as not to draw attention to themselves. ‘B’ listers make as much of a fuss as possible which makes them feel important.

‘A’ listers make their staff sign confidentiality agreements. ‘B’ listers hope that their staff have a contact at the tabloids.

When all said and done, every up and coming star wants to be on the elusive ‘A’ list. Alas few make it and even fewer once on it stay on it for long.

Run From fear and anchor to goal

No matter who you are or how famous you have become, there are only two real emotions in life, Pain and Pleasure. Of course, there are many other feelings that you can and will experience but when it comes down to it, all of the other feelings are based on either pain or pleasure.

Take for example the emotion that almost everyone feels at some time in their life and one which is a daily sensation for those who are in the public eye, self-doubt. Where is self-doubt based? This is rooted in pain; the pain which is felt through fear. The fear of not being good enough and not being able to live up to either your own or someone else's standards is painful.

What about the emotion of excitement or happiness? Again this is an emotion that many people feel and none feel as much as a celebrity. These emotions are based on pleasure which is expressed by love. The feelings of happiness and excitement come from loving what it is that you are doing and feeling confident that you will enjoy doing what it is you are doing.

So, if everything we feel is based on either pain or pleasure then it is clear that these two emotions are driving us forward or holding us back. It is amazing but the things that hold us back from being who we want to be can often be exactly the same as those that can motivate us to be that very same as those that can motivate us to be that very same person. Both pain and pleasure can be motivators and de-motivators.

It is pretty obvious why pain can hold us back; if we do

not want to feel physical or emotional pain then we avoid doing anything or being in certain situations that will cause us to feel it. If this happens then it is obvious that this will hold us back.

But pain can also push us forward. Ask two people why they get out of their bed every morning and go to work. One might answer that he or she works because of the pleasure they get from doing their job. This person is working at whatever he or she works at because of the enjoyment they get from doing what it is they do. Getting paid for it is almost a by product which gives them the income they need to pay for the outgoing expenses, with enough money left over to have the social life they want. Another person might answer that he or she is in the job that they are in because if they didn't have a job that paid the desired salary, then they would not be in a position to pay the outgoing expenses and are probably working so hard that they don't have time to spend whatever money remains on socialising.

The first person is driven by pleasure. People driven by pleasure do what they do because they enjoy it. Most people who go into acting begin by only wanting to act and the money is secondary. Of course, when the money starts flowing then it often becomes a very important part of the equation.

The second person is driven by pain. Their theory is that if they didn't have the job they wouldn't be able to pay their bills. The pain of not having money is what drives this person.

Both people get out of bed each morning and do the same day's work. But each are doing it for very different reasons and with completely different motives.

Another example would be people who are in intimate relationships or are married. If we asked two people why they were in the relationship one might say because of the pleasure it brings because they love the person and it is where they want to be. The other might say, or at least feel but not want to admit, that they are in the relationship because of the pain that not having a partner would bring. Being alone is not where they want to be. The first is driven to be in the relationship because of the emotion of pleasure and the second because of the emotion of pain. Which of these two relationships is likely to be fulfilling for the people involved? My guess is the one based on pleasure. On the face of it both of the people in the above example are in relationships but the reality is that only one is in the relationship because he or she wants to be there and not because they are afraid of the alternative.

This is where many people get confused with how to achieve fulfilment. They see the goal as being the important thing and forget about how they achieve it, especially when it comes to being famous. Often the only goal is to be famous and the journey to fame can be driven by pain or fear. If this is the case then once fame, no matter how it is achieved, is attained, then it becomes very unfulfilling. It is a reality that to be fulfilled with an achievement, the road to reaching the goal is as important if not more so that the goal itself.

If what you do is based on fear there is a real chance that you might miss the very goal that you want to succeed in. Fear pushes you in the general direction of the goal but as soon as challenges present themselves, as you move in the direction of the goal you are likely to be pushed off course. If on the other hand you are pulled towards your goal by love you are anchored to that goal and no matter how much you are pushed off course on the way to achieving the goal you will achieve it.

If a goal is based on fear then the first sign of challenging times might be enough to push you off course, and you would spend all of your energy just trying to stay on course.

Imagine you are on a boat. The wind is coming at you from the side and the tide is coming at you from the front just off centre. Your motor is at the back of your boat and is pushing you towards your port. The strain of the tide and the wind is really making it hard for you to reach the port and you need to alter direction all the time fighting against the elements just to stay on course. If the wind and tide are too strong for you then you may never make it to where you want to be. Now imagine you are the same boat with the same wind and tide. This time you have a heavy chain connected from your boat, which is anchored in the port you are headed for. The chain now winches you in. Do you get the picture? No matter how strong the wind or tide and no matter how much you drift off course, because you are connected and being pulled towards where you want to be, then there is no chance of you not getting there.

Ask yourself which of these two emotions drives you to achieve whatever it is in your life that you still want. Is it because you are anchored in what you really want, or is it because you are fearful of the alternative? Is your celebrity status as fulfilling as you thought it would be or does it lack something? What did you expect from what you have achieved? Often the only time we think about what we really want is when we run into problems and look for a way to solve the current challenges. By thinking ahead, and it's not too late now, then you can actually plan for the fulfilment that you may not have considered would be missing.

Let's not confuse fulfilment with having fun or being busy. I am sure most of us, when asked would admit that life has its fun times. However if the question was about having a fulfilled life then I am sure that many people would confess to having a certain amount of lacking in this area. It is very easy to be busy, especially when you are famous and have plenty of acquaintances around you all the time. For a while this is great fun and can create the illusion of being fulfilling. When reality kicks in however and you examine your life it becomes clear that what felt like fulfilment actually had little substance.

A fulfilling life has its foundation in pleasure. It is not possible to achieve personal fulfilment by going through life by making decisions based on the pain of not having something. You deserve a fulfilling life. You not only owe it to yourself to achieve the goals you want, you also owe it to yourself to enjoy the journey on the road to achieve your goals.

Inbuilt beliefs about money

Money has given me what I wanted or has it?

We all know people who have opinions about just about every aspect of life and who want, in fact feel it their duty, to share it with anyone and everyone who will listen. You may or may not be one of these opinionated people or you may not have opinions or thoughts about much of the great issues of life or even its trivia. But one thing I am certain that you will have an opinion on is money.

Let's not call it an opinion if that makes you feel uncomfortable, let's instead say that you have certain beliefs about money. I can imagine you are sitting there right now reading this and shaking your head telling yourself that you have no strong feelings about this touchy topic .... Well, you may think you don't but my guess is that in fact you do!

So now that I have convinced you or am about to convince you that you have some kind of belief about money let me make it clear why I am so sure that I am right. You see most of us have certain beliefs and quite frankly, most of the time we have no idea why we believe them. We have not taken the time to ponder the issues involved or sought the answers to any of the real questions that would help in the search for our true stance on many topics.

Much of what we believe is quite simply learned. Most of it is learned from our parents or from the people close to us when we were very young. We learn many of the beliefs that we hold as truths for much of our adult life before we reach the age of ten, with many of them being learned while we are still toddlers.

Many people grow up to have the same spiritual or religious beliefs as their parents and although some, when they are older, change their standpoint and so alter what they believe, it is more common than not for you to go through your whole adult life without changing what you believe, because you were taught it as a child, from what your parents believed when it comes to religion.

Similarly, your belief in money will often not change from the one your parents held dear. You may not even know what you think about having or not having money or about how money should be spent, but believe me you have an opinion. All I need to do to prove it to you would be to tell you that you would win ten million on the lottery today. You will have an opinion on what you are going to do with it or in many cases what it is going to do with you. Even if your opinion is that it will not change who you are or you will give it all away to charity, you have just made a decision on what you think about money, based on your built-in belief about it.

You might feel that money doesn't have too much bearing on who you are but again I urge you to have think about this. You may have enough money to allow you to live the life you want. If this is so then your belief about money is that it brings security.

I was once involved in a group discussion about money where I facilitated in bringing opinions and beliefs about money to the fore. I asked what people believed about money and if it was similar to what they had believed about money while they were growing up. In other words, was their belief an inherited belief or had they made a conscious decision to take time and think about what money meant to them as an individual. Most people in the group admitted that what they thought about money and how it affected their life and how they spent, saved or craved money was mainly due to what it was they had been taught as a child.

Below are some of the 'learned' beliefs that people shared with the group that day. Remember these are only beliefs which neither makes them true nor false statements.

"We have to struggle and strive to make money"
"Don't operate in debt"
"You never make sense of money no matter how much you actually have"
"Capitol is to be respected and profit is very important capitol"
"A penny saved is a penny earned"
"Enjoy the money you have"
"You never have enough"
"Money is something you don't talk about to anybody"
"If I don't save enough to take care of myself then I am a bad person"
"Money won't buy you happiness"
"You need to work your butt off for every penny you earn"
"Ignore money"
"Women especially don't understand money"
"You can't be honest and make money too"
"Everything comes down to money"
"I do what I have to for money but I do what I love for

nothing"

"Spending money is to be avoided"

"Money is for hoarding"

"Be frugal and save money"

"Be frivolous and spend impulsively"

"Pay the bills and save the rest"

"Work hard for a living and you will get by"

"Expect to be poor"

"If you don't have money you will be thought less of"

"We will always have enough money that we need"

"Hard work is the only way to be rewarded"

"If you get a good education you will make money"

"In the end it will all work out financially"

"You only need enough money to get by"

"Play it safe when it comes to money"

The important thing about all beliefs are that they are just that; our own personal belief. Just because you might believe something to be true does not in fact make it true. The same thing goes for your parents or whoever it was that was was fact, not only when it comes to money beliefs, but in all aspects of life, is only their own belief or opinion and may not actually be correct. Let's face it; they probably inherited what they believe to be true in life from their own parents. Truth is only an opinion and a truth of one person does not mean that it is the truth for everyone else. And the amazing thing about the whole idea about truth is that, just because someone doesn't agree with you or believe the same as you, it doesn't make your belief false. It is still your truth.

We all have our own beliefs about everything in life including money. Money is an easy way to demonstrate this fact, but it is equally true for just about any belief. A belief is just a personal opinion, and not only can another person believe something different from you but even if we believe something to be true today we can change our minds and believe something different at any point in the future. This is the whole point of gathering information and experiences about different subjects.

So even if you have held a certain belief close to you for a large part of your life, it is never too late to re-evaluate it and change your mind or make that same belief stronger by taking it as your own or changing it from what you thought to be true in the past.

What would it be like if you decided to live as if you had no money at all? How would that change you? Think about it. The obvious things would change such as you would not be able to go out as much and maybe not at all. You would not have the comfort of knowing you can buy luxuries as well as essentials.

But how would you as a person differ?

Most of us rely on money not only to buy things that we need and desire but also as a form of security. Our outlook on life and the future is often determined by how secure or insecure we are, and if money is one way of bringing security to your life then what would happen if you didn't have it any more.

To get to understand yourself more fully try simplifying your life a bit and cut out the frills. Bring yourself back to the bare essentials. I am not a nudist, but I do know people who are. They say that by getting rid of clothes they are free to understand themselves more fully because everyone around them is the same. It is that kind of simplification that I mean for you to try. Not nudism but the simplification of 'getting rid of' excess stuff that you don't really need. By doing this you will start to see yourself a little bit better and understand your wants and needs more fully without the security of having everything you want in your life.

I am not suggesting that you give all your money away, but it might be possible for you to make a commitment to yourself that you do not spend more than is absolutely essential for one month. Pay attention during that time as to what happens to your social life such as entertaining people at your house or going out. How many new friends do you make when you cannot attend openings and events? How many people don't come to see you as much because you are not treating them? What do you learn about how you find things to do when you can't just jump in the car and fill it up with fuel? Do you take more walks? This in turn might make you fitter. Do you pick and choose more vegetables to eat because of the price of the more basic food? How is your mind and soul affected now that you are not concerning yourself with the social issues of keeping up with the Joneses?

Food for thought isn't it? How much do you rely on money as security? It is good to have a reserve of everything in your life including money. Believe me, I am not knocking having money. In fact I am saying it is a good thing if thought about and used in the right way. It is good for your personal fulfilment and positive thinking for the future to have a reserve of money. But don't let all your happiness depend on having it because, like any dependency, if it is ever not there your whole life will crumble.

Money can be a weapon. When you have enough money or more than enough money you are virtually in no emotional or physical danger. The power that having money gives us, when used as a weapon, makes us feel that we are not at risk from anything. But when we start to have financial challenges then it stops being about money and starts to be about survival both physically and emotionally. Worrying about money can make you crazy and if you go into survival mode then it is not about money at all, it is about you as a person.

People who use money as a weapon often start to define themselves by their money. Wealthy people can often influence politics by giving donations to political parties. Owners of newspapers and television companies use their money and power to try to influence their readers' and viewers' thoughts.

Surely a healthier way to think about money is as a tool for your life. When you think of it like this then you are able to get what you most want in life without much of the stuff that holds you back. Using money as a tool you will be able to use your money to leverage and create the future you want for yourself and not as a way to influence those around you.

The problem is that many people don't like to talk about money, especially their own money. People don't like talking about their own money because they think it is either no one else's business or because they are embarrassed about how much of it they have.

I recently spoke at a seminar where there were about five hundred people attending. I asked for those who would like to win £10 million on the lottery to put their hands up. About two hundred raised their hands. I then asked if anyone who had not put there hand up, i.e. did not want to win £10 million on the lottery, would give a reason for their decision. One man said it was because it was far too much money for one person to have and said it was vulgar to have as much money as that, especially when there were people with no money and starving in the world. I asked for a show of hands from the people who had not put their hands up, asking them if they agreed with this man and if this was the reason they had not put their hands up. Of the three hundred who had not originally put their hands up about two hundred and ninety put their hands up in agreement with what the man had said.

What was going on in these people's heads? Was it guilt? Was it fear of being branded rich? No, it was simply that their belief system was holding them back from thinking it through. I shared with them that I would love to win £10 million. And I asked then that before they judged me for wanting it, that they listen to what I would do with the money.

I would pay off my mortgage and buy each of my children a new car. I would also put some money away for a rainy day. I shared with them that doing that would probably account for about £300,000. I would then donate £9.7 million to local charities.

Suddenly the three hundred or so people who originally did not want the money wanted it. They could see that their original belief about money, which was probably 'I need to keep every penny I have for myself' could be altered. They suddenly saw money as a tool to be used for good instead of a weapon to be used for selfish gain. What are you doing with your money? Are you using it wisely and in a way that feels right to you? Or are you hindered by your old learned beliefs regarding what you should do with money?

Have - Do - Be

When I work with individuals on a one-to-one basis I tend to come across people who fall into one of the following two categories. They either have a specific goal or challenge which they want help in achieving or they have no real goal or challenge in mind but just know that where they are in their life right now is not where they want to be.

Many people break their lives down into sections, work, family, social, fun, community and so on. They attempt to satisfy themselves in only one or two of these areas and neglect the rest. At best this can mean success in only one or two parts of their life and at worst a total disaster because of an unbalanced and unfulfilling life.

If the person has a challenge that comes into the category of not having any real goal then I often find he or she will say something like, "I just want to be the person that I know I really am". OK that sounds pretty logical and straightforward, but what is not so obvious is the route that is often taken in an attempt to be who they want to be. They have no real concept of what just being themselves really involves.

I believe that in the search for oneself many people go about it in a very back to front way. I call it the 'Have–Do–Be' syndrome. Simply put, many people, in their search to find themselves, follow this route, which is in actual fact completely the reverse of how to truly find the real you.
'If only I had xxxxxxxx then it would allow me to do the things I want to do which in turn would allow me to be the person I know I am' is one of the phrases I hear most often when I work

on this with clients. They substitute xxxxxxxx with something that they feel is the thing that is holding them back from being the real them.

'If only I had more money then it would allow me to do the things I want to do because I could afford it, which in turn would allow me to be the person know I am'

They justify the fact that they want more money in their life with the idea that only with more money would they be ably to be who they want to be and live the life which reflects themselves well. They don't see how they can ever let the real them shine until they have the thing they feel is lacking and holding them back.

'If only I had money then it would allow me to do the things I want to do which in turn would allow me to be the person I know I am'

'If only I had a partner then it would allow me to do the things I want to do which in turn would allow me to be the person I know I am'

'If only I had fame then it would allow me to do the things I want to do which in turn would allow me to be the person I know I am'

Putting the emphasis on having is putting the emphasis on things instead of on yourself. There is nothing at all wrong in wanting things in your life, nothing wrong in that at all, but when you begin to think that having this thing is going to magically help you achieve being the person you think you really are then you have it all back to front.

It is only when you can be the person you really are all the time, with or without certain things in your life, that you will allow yourself to do the things you want to do which in turn will make sure you attract and have the things in your life that you want. You see it is by turning the whole have–do–be formulae on its head that you begin to see the real power in finding your real authentic self.

When you place the emphasis on external things while you are in the process of searching for internal truths then you immediately give away your biggest asset, you give away your own power. By giving your power over to the things you want that you think will help you achieve the goal, you are putting yourself in a position of lacking control over your future. In fact you are giving your control to external sources. These things that you thought were going to make your life perfect and allow you to shine as a person, can disappear from your life as fast as they entered, and when they do the life you have built round about them often collapses too because it is not sustainable or built on a strong foundation based on your personal values.

Often it is a delaying excuse that makes people wait for things before allowing the real self to shine. Can you imagine what would have happened if some of the world's greats had waited until they had all the things they wanted in their life before allowing themselves to live the life they knew they could? What would have happened if Mother Teresa had waited until she had had enough money in place before she decided that being her true and authentic self was to work with the underprivileged children of the world? Her work would probably never have got off the ground. She decided just to be herself first which allowed her to do the things in life that she wanted to do and I am sure if you could ask her today she would tell you that by doing it she had all that she ever wanted in life.

'Have-Do-Be' is closely connected to people who think with the 'if only' mentality. Have-Do-Be people will tell themselves that if only they had a certain thing in their life, love, more money, a different job, more time .... then it would allow them to do the things they want to in their life, which in turn would allow them to be the person they really want to be. A real situation might go something like this; If only I could win the lottery (have) then I could give a lot of money to under privileged people (do) and that would make me feel better because it would be in alignment with who I really am (be). This all sounds plausible but there is a basic flaw with this way of thinking, which is that the 'being' who you really want to be is totally reliant on the external situations which you have no control over. Winning the lottery is not under your control and so you are back to relying on factors that you are not in charge of to determine your future.

By turning the whole Have-Do-Be thing on its head and making it Be-Do-Have you will be in total control of everything you want, including your future. By being true to yourself and living your life in line with your real values and your authentic self, you will live your life by being the person you really are which will allow you the total freedom to do the things you want to in your life. This in turn lets you have the life you want. The real life situation here would go something like this; by being (be) your authentic self and genuinely caring for under privileged people, without any other reason but because you care, you will be able to help them in a real way (do) by giving of yourself instead of giving money, (which you probably could afford to do without in the first place) which in turn will allow you to have an inner piece of mind and a total sense of fulfilment (have) for what you have done.

Many people live a life that is not in line with who they really are. There are many reasons why this might be the case; pressure from peers, parents, or yourself. You want to just give up your work and go work with underprivileged people, but, yes there is always a 'but', and that but might be other people, yourself, the lifestyle you enjoy or something else. Whatever it is it is stopping you living your life as you really want to so you revert to Have-Do-Be instead of Be-Do-Have.

It is often said by people who feel they might have acted differently in a given situation, that with hindsight they would have done things another way. By thinking like this they are, in a way excusing themselves for their actions, which is unnecessary if they acted to the best of their ability. While excusing themselves may help make them feel better about what has happened the reality is that the past cannot be altered, no matter how hard they try. People who think like this and live in the past tend to be living with an 'if only' attitude to life; If only I had done this differently........ If only I had more money .... If only I had had a better childhood ..... If only I got that promotion last week ..... If only I was famous .... and so on.

Hindsight by its very nature can only be observational, which, as we have established cannot be changed. With this in mind it is equally important to acknowledge that it is in fact possible to have the future be just as we want. While the past will be a factor in shaping both the physical and emotional parts of who we are and what our present situation is, it cannot be allowed to determine our future. We are the masters of our own destiny and if we are inclined to use hindsight as a tool in helping shape our actions, how much more important would foresight be in creating our future?

This is not intended to mean looking into the future to see what is going to happen; instead foresight is about determining one's future by clearly seeing and creating the path ahead. It is about acknowledging that you are in the present, which has been shaped, in part by your past, and that your future can be as you want it to be.

In reality many people simply leave most major decisions to chance. It is simpler just to wait and see what the world throws at us and then use our 'fire fighting' skills to fight our way through life. Have you ever stopped to imagine what life would be like if there were no fires to put out? If you were so in tune with where you were going that you could see any obstacles that were approaching before they even appeared?

Often we attempt to do things the wrong way round in life; like the old saying 'putting the cart before the horse'. Would you ever consider putting a large hat on your head before pulling on a tight top? Probably not and if you did you would find it difficult at best and downright impossible at worst. But so many of us do just that with our own lives, then say, in hindsight, I would have put the top on first or 'If only' I had put the top on first ....

How does this relate to real life? The 'if only'

syndrome does not only occur when people look back to the past it can often be used with the present or the future in mind.

If only I was wealthier, then all my problems would be solved

If only I had a partner, then I would be happy

If only I were slimmer.... taller ..... healthier .... smarter.... more talented......... the list is endless.

By eliminating this way of thinking you will begin to focus on the future in a totally different and much more positive way.

Try this for yourself. Simply start living every moment of every day just being you. Not the person other people think you are or the person others or yourself expect you to be, just pure and simply <u>be</u> you. You will soon find that you are <u>doing</u> the things you love to do without much effort and attracting the things you want in your life so that you <u>have</u> all that you want in life.

Self Talk

Talking is great, in fact it is one of my favourite pastimes. It is one of the most common ways for humans to communicate with each other on a day-to-day level. Before the inventions of worldwide communication systems such as radio, television, telephones and email we were restricted in how we were able to reach to people in our immediate vicinity. Now we can be heard around the world and beyond, giving us the power to influence others in far off places by what we say. Verbalising our thoughts can indeed be a powerful tool.

There are many different ways to talk. We may verbalise what we have on our minds to other people by making a few well constructed sounds come out of our mouths and we communicate with them. We may also communicate inaudibly to others and to ourselves without uttering a word.

Most of us love to talk. It is a way of expressing ourselves; a way to get across our thoughts to those who are around us so that they can understand exactly what we have on our minds. The problem with talk is that it can very easily be misunderstood and often is, especially when we are trying to communicate something important with others. How often have you had a thought in your head and tried to communicate it to someone else, only for them to misunderstand what you were saying and get the wrong end of the stick.

It is important to remember that talking and communicating are two very different things. Other things come into it when you successfully communicate what you have on your mind. Body language and tonality are two of the most important. It is very difficult for anyone to really understand what you are saying unless you accompany words with some of the other signals that go along with language.

So, it is important that other people accurately understand what you arc trying to say to them. It goes without saying that if it is possible for others to misinterpret what you are saying to them, then it is equally feasible that you may misunderstand what they have to say to you. I don't think many people would agree that it is easy to misunderstand others. The thing that many people may not have considered is that it is actually possible to talk to yourself in such a way that you miss the point of what you are trying to say.

Self-talk can be one of the greatest tools you have in motivating yourself into doing something. When you have a big audition or have to increase your comfort zone, you will often self talk in a way that you build yourself up in preparation for the event. If possible you will also, before such an occasion, find others who will feed you positive information. You may be going for a photo shoot and so may look for someone close to you to reassure you and tell you that you look great. You may be reading for a part or appearing on a show and you want someone to run over your lines with you and tell you that you will be fantastic. Finding others to encourage you through verbal motivation is important to build confidence in you.

In the same way you will spend many minutes, hours or even days in the ritual of positive self talk. A practice that helps give yourself the necessary confidence that will allow you to be at your peak when the time comes. All in all positive self talk is invaluable.

Is it possible that you also practice in negative self-talk? In fact I think that those of us who do this really indulge ourselves in something that is quite macabre. We say things to ourselves that we would not allow anyone else, not even our closest soul mate say to us. Have you ever thought to yourself, which is the same as talking to your self, 'oh I am so stupid'?

Name calling to yourself is one of the strangest things that humans do. We would not allow a friend to talk to us the way we often talk to ourselves. If they did the friendship would surely be very short lived. Can you imagine how long you would remain friends with someone who repeatedly calls you stupid? Yet you will, I am sure sometimes call yourself this or something similar. Each time you call yourself names a part of you believes it just a little bit more than the last time you called your self the name. then before you know it you actually believe you are stupid.

Stop name calling yourself. It is a bad habit which is very damaging to you.

Famous Because You Are Insecure
Or Insecure Because You Are Famous

It is one of these questions. You know, like the one I mentioned earlier; what came first the chicken or the egg? It has been debated and argued over many times and the wonderings of insecurity and fame evoke similar discussion.

Over the years I have been around many famous people. Some were world famous stars and others local heroes. The one thing I noticed in the vast majority, but by no means all of them, was that there was a certain degree of insecurity lurking somewhere in their being.

The question is, was this insecurity there from a young age and indeed the thing that motivated the person to strive for approval through adoring fans and fame. Or were they secure in themselves before their celebrity status showed up and the constant attention made them insecure.

Ask the celebrity to their face and they would probably deny any insecurity exists, but just watch as soon as a bad review is printed in the local or national rag about them or when one of their peers is offered a job over them and you will see that insecurity is never far away

Insecurity is often the thing that drives celebrities onwards. Security for most of us is being in our comfort zone with everything we need and want round about us. This is the thing that is lacking with celebrities, even the ones that look as if they have everything they ever need. The fact is that fame has no upper limit. There is never a stage in any person's rise to fame where they are safe from the clutches of sudden disaster. There are many examples of people who, one minute are amongst the highest paid movie stars in the world, and the next they are unhireable. Insecurity sets in as soon as a star feels he or she has lost control of their own destiny. Just as the insecure child looks to a parent for praise and approval, an insecure star looks to his fans for that same source of comfort. When it's not there then self doubt, fear and more insecurity follows.

Why are some people insecure?

Basically, insecurity comes from not knowing. Not knowing if people will like you, not knowing what the future holds for you, not knowing if you are god enough. There are a few things you can do to help boost your security. The main one is to take your own fate into your own hands. Having the confidence to know that even if others don't approve of you or the things you do, you still believe in yourself, brings security. Knowing that you are well prepared, and that if you are not received well is more to do with you not being right for the situation than a slur on your ability, builds your security. Keep in mind that you are doing, and always will do the best you can, and you will be able to top up your self confidence and keep insecurity at bay.

Attention Seeking

It's one of these things that most of us do. We all want it; Attention! From a newborn baby to an elderly pensioner, we all seek attention.

As infants and toddlers, we cry and throw tantrums and soon learn that by doing this we get some kind of attention. Not always the attention we were seeking as a tantrum can and often does bring out less than our parents' best. But the upside is that we do get ourselves noticed. So we learn from an early age that attention is relatively simple to get. By the time we reach our teens we have refined our attention seeking skills a little and realise that there are ways to get the right kind of attention. We realise that by attracting the wrong kind of attention we are noticed for all the wrong reasons. We soon realise that the satisfaction we get from receiving the right kind of attention is much more rewarding than when we are noticed for all the wrong reasons. Tantrums bring the wrong type of attention. Being talented or practiced at something brings not only attention but also admiration and often praise. Yes, this type of attention feels much better. It also does the ego good to have people tell you that they enjoy what you do. So you thought you were trying to attract the attention of other people for your own self gratification when in fact the very people you are trying to attract attention from are seeking to be with you anyway. Yes this is a much more enjoyable way of getting attention.

So we learn that there is good attention and bad attention and in actual fact the good attention takes less energy to achieve than throwing a tantrum.

Attention is one of these things that while we seek it, it is fun and exciting, but when it is unwanted we complain that we have no privacy. The problem is that when we are known to seek attention, and fame brings attention to you even if you don't want it or seek it, then it is almost impossible to turn off. Other people feel it is their right to claim part of you all the time just because for some of the time you wanted and went out of your way to seek their attention. A quiet private dinner with a close friend turns into a media frenzy. A stroll on the beech with a loved one degenerates into a hideous exhibition of hide and seek with you being the sought.

But now it's different. You realise that attention is not something that can be turned off and on at a whim. The attention you attract is not only related to the things that you do but also to who you are. Even if you are doing nothing, which ordinarily should get you any attention, when you become *someone* you attract attention when you are doing the most mundane of things.

Now it seems that the tables have turned and that other people seek your attention. Fans want to be noticed by you. They stop you in the supermarket, in clothes shops, when you are walking down the street. They want your attention. They feel they know you well enough to demand it from you. But you don't want it, at least not at that precise moment. You do want it, in fact you need it, but you only want it when it suits you. Here's the bad news; it rarely works like that.

Once fame comes your way you will have the attention you so badly craved in your early years but now it is not for you to decide from when and where the attention comes. Nor are you able to control the type of attention you create.

As I mentioned earlier, you realised at a young age that you could attract good and bad attention by your behaviour. Throw a tantrum and it often led to bad attention in the form of a scolding from your parent. Sing a song for your parents' friends and you attracted praise and good attention. Now you are learning that the same rules apply as an adult. Star in a blockbuster film with an outstanding performance and you will attract the praise and rewarding attention you seek. Fall out of a nightclub drunk and incoherent and the attention you attract will feel one hundred times worse than the scolding you received as a child for the tantrum.

The trick to handling this two edged sword that can fill you with delight or cut you to shreds is attitude. Learn that when you are a public figure you are going to attract attention whether you want to or not. You will not be in control of the form of the attention in so much that you are only human and while you may not fall out of a bar at 2am you will inevitably do something which others will perceive as being noteworthy for the wrong reasons. Your attitude towards such publicity or attention is vital to how the attention you get in the future will pan out.

There are many recorded incidents of a well known face handling bad attention in the wrong way. It has been reported that Prince William allegedly hit a photographer for taking a picture of him coming out of a nightclub or celebrities pushing photographers out of their way at airports. Then there are the ones who seem to endear themselves to the attention seekers. Kate Price as Jordan is well used to being glamorous in front of a camera but it seems she also doesn't mind the odd picture being taken of her looking less than her best. The unwanted attention Hugh Grant received when he was arrested for picking up a lady of the night in Hollywood could have ruined his career as a cute, rather fumbling actor. But it didn't. Why not? Because of the differing attitudes to the attention they got.

Some famous people think they have a right to be able to turn on and off the attention at will. Maybe they are right. Maybe they should be able to dictate when and where they are public property, open to scrutiny only when they choose. The reality is that this doesn't happen. It may be right or not but it happens. It is how you deal with it that is important.

Grant and Price remain in control. They probably realise that they are going to get attention whether they want or seek it or not. So, they have decided that the best thing to do is be honest and use it to their advantage.

Prince Harry did himself no favours by flying off the handle when he got unwanted attention while Hugh Grant came out of his episode of unwanted attention probably more popular than before.

Being prepare
towards the attention
more possible to hav

ZAYN YOLANDA
SITUATION

Famous for the wrong reasons

You will no doubt have heard the phrase "any publicity is good publicity". While that is often the case it is not always true.

There have been many occasions where people have first come to the attention of the public for the wrong reasons. While some undoubtedly relish in the fact that the cameras are pointing towards them and don't seem to care why, others would see the unwelcome invasion of privacy something to stay well away from.

For the ordinary man or woman to be thrust into public glare, the sudden shock of attention can be overwhelming. One minute they are Mr. or Ms. unrecognizable from somewhere and the next, their face is being flashed up on our television screens and in newspapers and their life story told to the world. People suddenly recognise you in the street. It gets difficult to do simple things like go shopping or go about your normal daily business. You're recognised anywhere and everywhere that you go. Now I am sure that this can be fun for a while but if the unwanted attention continues for longer than just a few days then tempers may fray at the imposition into your personal life. This of course is just what the tabloids and journalists are looking for. They want to continue the headline with more headlines and when you lose your temper in front of them that's exactly what they have, It simply gives them something else to report. Like it or not this is what sells papers and increases viewing figures.

You would imagine that for the celebrity, being in the

...light for whatever reason would be good. After all your celebrity status requires that people talk about you and that you're seen on the television and in newspapers. I would hazard a guess that John Leslie, O.J. Simpson, Michael Barrymore, Hugh Grant and Michael Jackson would tell you in no uncertain terms that they would have rather have the front-page headlines that each of them have for alleged misdemeanours.

There are usually five emotions or stages that the person will go through when they feel, rightly or wrongly, that they have been misjudged.

The first is an anger followed by fear then frustration, insecurity and revenge. There are obviously many more emotions mixed in with these and sometimes if lucky, a sixth emotion can be tacked on at the end, which is forgiveness and understanding.

Unfortunately, often this emotion is short lived and anger can follow again soon after. If this happens then professional help may be needed to get past what has happened

The anger that is felt is usually directed towards the accusers. Sometimes this will be a stranger, other times it will be friends or even a family member who you feel has wronged you. The closer the person or the situation is to you the more anger may be felt. When the story, whatever it might be gets out, there may be a second wave of people to be angry with. Did your employer, clients and colleagues stand by you or did they join with the accusers and treat you as guilty before you could defend yourself?

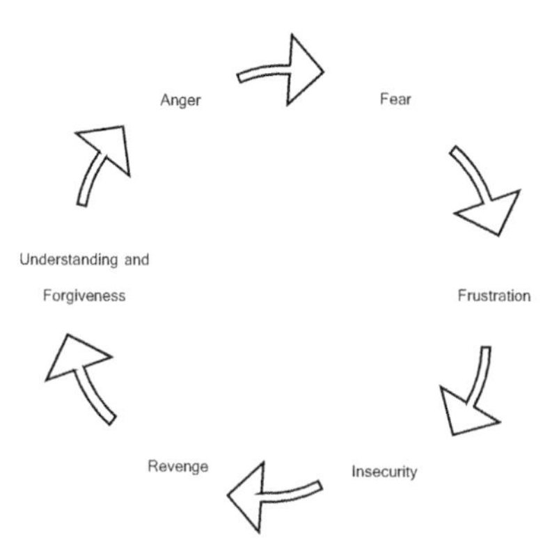

Then of course you may also be angry at 'the system'. If you are accused of something and the police are involved then 'the system' means the law of the land and all that that entails. If it was something which was not illegal like dating your best friend's girlfriend then 'the system' may be the social system which you are usually a part of. This stage of being angry is often a counter productive one because the angrier you are the less people want to be around you, and the more journalists will be attracted to you and want to report on your temper tantrums. Remember they want to sell papers and increase viewer figures and you dealing with your dilemma well will not do that. Behaving badly and smashing a few paparazzi cameras or falling out of a nightclub hardly able to stand gives them something juicy to report.

But anger is indeed usually the first stage. It comes and hopefully goes quickly and how you deal with that will determine how you cope with the next few stages.

Then comes fear. Panic attacks, waking in the middle of the night and feeling a real sense of being alone, only adds to the fear that you feel. Fear comes from uncertainty and the fear of the unknown can be overpowering. You may worry about the unknown reaction you get from others; what they really think and feel about what has or is alleged to have happened. A celebrity will fear for his or her future because they will be unsure if they will come out of this looking good, bad or indifferent.

Hugh Grant, after he was arrested for picking up a prostitute in Los Angeles, must have wondered how the public, his fans, his girlfriend and the film studios would react.

Amazingly, even though he was arrested and hideous pictures of him were plastered all over the worldwide press, his career was actually enhanced by what had happened. He was front page news for all the wrong reasons and despite this his career went from strength to strength. His relationship however did not survive, although one wonders how it was before, if he felt the need to pick someone up from the street.

High earning celebrities will also fear the financial implications of unwanted publicity. The television companies, record companies and film studios will assess the situation and come down on one of two sides of the fence. They will either love the idea that you have managed to achieve huge publicity and try to capitalise on it or they will see it as an excuse to release you from any existing contracts you have with them without compensation. The old saying "the bigger you are the harder you fall" is certainly true in the high-flying world of show business. A local celebrity will find bad publicity hard to handle. A national star usually has more to lose than a local celebrity; both will, however, usually get through the ordeal fine. Unfortunately for the global star there will often be nowhere to hide.

Frustration comes after fear. If you have appeared in the papers for the wrong reasons, one of your biggest challenges will be to rebuild your life and career. The frustration is magnified and multiplied if you're actually not guilty of what you're being accused of doing. The fight to clear your name can become an obsession and overtake everything else in your life. The need to get justice is a strong driving force and many people have not come out so well after having taken the wrongdoers and accusers on. Financially it can be bad news as well as having a bad effect on you as an individual. You may even come out of the frustration stage looking worse than when you went in.

Frustration also emphasises the sense that you are not able to do anything about the situation. Many people, including your fans, family and friends may feel that there is no smoke without fire and on some occasions they're right. But for the celebrity who is wrongly accused and gets caught up in the frenzy of tabloid reporting it can be a lifetime project to clear your name. It may even seem that the more you deny something the guiltier you appear.

After frustration comes insecurity. Those who you once considered your friends have to be looked upon as being potential enemies. It is not unknown for best friends to sell their story to the papers for cash, no matter how dubious the link. Insecurity can also mean that you turn to and trust the people you shouldn't. People that under normal circumstances you would keep a wide berth of suddenly become your closest friends. Insecurity is an imbalance of what you perceive to be reality and fantasy. Not knowing who to trust will often lead you to making decisions you would not normally make, and which are not in your best interest either personally or professionally. This is a time for you to gather close those you know and have been able to trust in the past, and even though you may not feel you can trust them one hundred percent they're a better bet than strangers.

Then the ugly emotion of revenge raises its head. I say ugly because there are few occasions when revenge will be the right thing to do. It may feel good at that time and in the short term make you feel better about the situation but in the longer-term revenge is destructive. Some people may decide to act on the feeling of revenge and get it out of their system but even if you don't act out your revenge, keeping it inside will eat you up and could destroy you. Work on getting rid of this potentially harmful emotion and getting yourself focused on what really matters.

Here are three ways to overcome some of these emotions.

1. Gather your trusted friends around you. Take time to regroup and talk to people you trust.

2. Face your fears. Don't hide them away because they would just raise themselves sometime in

the future. Most probably when you least expect them to and when you are least able to do anything about them.

3. Focus on yourself and your career. Try to forget that you are a celebrity and get back to being yourself. Remember that being a celebrity is what you do it is not who you are.

Learn From Your Mistakes

This next section will be relevant to you if you are not famous or at any of the three stages of fame.

"Will I never learn?"

Now there is a statement I bet you have said a thousand times. I'm sure you have and believe me, you are not the only one. It is a strange thing but most of us seem to have great difficulty in learning. I don't mean conventional learning, for example studying for an exam or finding out information for an assignment. I mean learning from past experiences and making sure that once we have gone through a bad experience, and after saying "never again", we learn from that experience and don't actually do it again. We often just do not learn and yes, we do it again, and sometimes again and again and again.

When might we say 'will I never learn' to ourselves?

Possibly it could be after a relationship split. Do you remember saying it? "Men/Women! Who needs them? I'll never do that again. In reality most of us do.

It may be that you have been out on the town one Saturday night and had, as they say, one too many. When you wake up the next day, what did you say? "Never again" By the time Saturday comes around again you seem to have forgotten the way you felt before and repeated the whole never again experience all over again.

Or you may have said it after that extra spicy meal you had which almost took the skin off the roof of your mouth. But what happens? The next time you're in the situation that someone is having the same dish, you try just a little bit. What are you thinking? Do you imagine the chef missed out the spice this time? I don't think so.

Or you may have a business partner, or friend who has let you down once too often? You convince yourself that you will never let anyone close enough to you to let that ever happen again. More often than not you do.

The fact is we do learn from our mistakes. We do know that we don't want to be hurt or let down or humiliated in that way again. The hard thing is to use the learning experience in a positive way to help ensure the next time is different. The next time may not be perfect but if we have learned properly it will be better than the last time. This sounds all too sensible I hear you say. Well, you're right, it is about sense, common sense. You can't go through life shying away from things just because you tried before, and it turned out wrong. Nor can you go through life not trusting each other because of the actions of a former lover, business partner or friend. You can use these past negative experiences, learn from them and turn them into future positive situations.

There are no easy answers or magic remedies but let's think about how so called passed mistakes can be learned from. Use the following to ask yourself some questions about situations instead of looking for the answers.

The Basics

When a baby is born it has no option but to put its full trust in its parents. Even if it could decide not to have faith in them I don't think it would. Why? Because it doesn't have any past experiences of its parents letting it down. It is only as the child grows that it learns from both good and bad encounters with people and situations. If the child goes too close to a fire and gets burnt, it will be more careful in the future. Granddad always gives the child lots of attention, so it goes back for more. In this way the child grows up knowing the difference between good experiences and bad ones. The strange thing is that even though we grow up knowing the difference between these experiences we don't always seem to learn from them.

Let me put it another way. We are sometimes easily drawn into a false sense of security by promises made by others. Let's imagine that the child had an uncle who was a bit of a grumpy person and maybe even behaved in a nasty way to the child. Can you believe that a five-year-old would stay away from him, even if it knew he was a bit grumpy or nasty, if he was holding a bag of its favourite sweets? Possibly the first time of offering it would. Maybe even the second time, but after a while the bad times don't seem so bad and the good things, the sweets in this case, are too much of a lure to be ignored.

We all can be like children because for most of us trusting others is the most natural thing in the world. Then one day we find ourselves in a situation where that trust or understanding is shattered. When this happens, most people take a long time to trust anyone again. As time goes by and as many different things go on in our lives the bad experiences seem to fade slightly, and the promise of good times ahead becomes irresistible. Why don't you take a few minutes of your time right now just to think of some of the ‘never again’ situations you have been in and ask yourself if you have gone into a similar situation again.

Sex, Love, Relationships and Fame

Relationships

There a many funny illustrations of 'never again' situations in relationships but there are also many very serious situations to do with relationships that some people find themselves in.

There is the situation of the abusive partner, both men and women, who verbally, physically or emotionally are cruel to their partner. This can be a very serious problem for the person on the receiving end. No one can really understand the problem if they have not had to experience it first hand. We can empathise and sympathise but to actually understand it is impossible if you have not actually been through it yourself. Those people who are fortunate enough not to have been victim of a violent partner or parent can hardly comprehend what goes on inside the mind of the person who is being beaten or abused. We say things that are meant to be well comprehend what goes on inside the mind of the person who is being beaten or abused. We say things that are meant to be well intended but are usually totally misguided like, 'just leave him/her, I would.'

Well, I wonder, would we? It is an easy statement to make but not so easy for many victims to carry out. Other well intended advice might be "Go to the police" or "Why don't you go to a relationship councillor?"

There are so many people who are hit when their partner comes home drunk at the weekend and it happens time and time again. It seems logical to outsiders that the easiest option is to leave. So why on earth don't the victims leave? In many situations the reason they don't up and leave is the security.

Security? What security I hear you ask? Yes, many people find security, even in bad situations.

The fact that they have a roof over their head and usually money to put food on the table is, for some people, a secure enough reason for putting up with a horrendous situation. The fact that the children have a place to live can often be an over riding factor. It's better than being homeless or in a hostel. Or they may stay with their partner because they feel that the whole situation is their own fault, when in reality it clearly is not. Guilt, or the feeling of guilt, can make them do things which seem strange and unthinkable to the outsider looking in. They start thinking strange thoughts sometimes. They may even feel they can change the bad behaviour of the partner. This more often than not never happens.

Eventually many victims of abusive relationships do make the break and leave. Now here is where the learning part comes in. In many situations the next relationship that this person enters into is with someone else who treats them in exactly the same way. Or they go back to their original partner after a while. This, to the onlooker can be baffling.

We must be careful not to judge them if and when they do go back because as I pointed out earlier, we all do it. Maybe not in such a dramatic fashion, but by saying never again and then going back on it, we do the same thing much of the time. What we must hope is that the person has learned from their past situation and will use the knowledge gained to improve the future. Later I will explain how we might be able to do this.

Not all relationships are stormy or are bad because of violence. Sometimes it can be lack of communication that is the cause of a poor relationship. Why do some people marry three or four times? No one goes into a marriage thinking it will only last for a short time. We all expect it to be for life. If the first marriage was bad because of poor communication then you would think the next time that person would do their best to find a partner where the communication is good. It is often the case that the communication the second and third time around is as poor as it was the first. So why then do they seem to fall into the same situation each time? Security, yes we covered that, but what else might it be? Sometimes the bad memories of a situation fade and do not seem as bad as they actually were. It may be that they feel they are a stronger person than before, more able and better equipped to deal with the same type of situation should it arise. Positive thinking is excellent, but this alone may not be enough to change things for the future and may leave you wide open to be in a similarly bad situation again.

While the situations I have mentioned above are bad enough for the ordinary person, just imagine the hardship that would be suffered by someone who lives their life in the limelight. The pain and pressures of this can sometimes be so great that the person it is happening to simply gives up or turns to self abuse.

How then can you use bad situations in a positive way?

Try now to think of a situation, not necessarily a relationship issue, in which you have found yourself previously and that you have said 'never again'. Try to make it a little incident which is not too serious if you can.

Ask yourself now if you have entered into a similar situation again. If the answer is no, then ask if it is because:

1. That particular situation has not cropped up again.
2. The situation has cropped up again but because you haven't dealt with your feelings from the last time yet you have stayed clear of entering into it again.
3. You learned from last time and were strong enough not to go back there again.

Write in your own reason.

If the answer is 1 then it is important you try to deal with it before you find yourself faced with a similar set of circumstances again. Similarly with answer 2; by staying out of a situation that is similar to a bad one you had in the past until you have had time to learn and recover from the last one is the correct thing to do. If the answer is 3.....well done!

If the answer is yes then ask yourself the following

1. Was it because you were better prepared this time?
2. Was the 'never again' statement you said to yourself after the first time unfounded?
3. Are you asking yourself why you let yourself back into a similar situation again.

If the answer was 1 and you were better prepared for it, how did you prepare for it?

Write down in your diary or journal how you dealt with it? With many of the more serious situations you may need professional help in the form of counselling to come to terms with the past, but for some of the smaller instances you will be able to deal with it yourself, and then you will feel more confident trying to sort out the more difficult problems. Use the fact that you learned from your bad past experiences to give yourself a pat on the back. And remember to reward yourself for this.

I am a great believer in writing things down, or in my case scribbling things down.

So let's start by doing just that. Write down a 'never again' situation you want to deal with right now. Then write down the thoughts you were having and the feelings you were going through during that time. The feelings you were having towards the thing or person who was causing the problem for you. (That may have been yourself of course) Make notes of the feelings you were having towards the situation itself and the feelings you were having towards yourself at the time. Record your emotions. Were you feeling angry, frustrated, annoyed, hurt or let down?

Then write down the outcome of that particular episode in your life. For instance, did it hurt you? Did you run from it? Did you try to fight it? Did you secretly enjoy the challenge?

After you have done this, write down 'the last straw' the thing that made you say 'never again.' This may be difficult and I think it is important to take your time finding out what the last straw for you actually was, even if you need to sleep on it before answering. It is important that you know what happened to make you say never again, because it is at that point that you may have felt defeated. You were not defeated, but you may have felt it. Record things from the most insignificant situation like the food which was too spicy or the times you gave up trying to ice skate because you kept falling, to more serious problems, the hurts and let downs you suffered because of other people.

Was it embarrassment that caused you to say, no more? Were people laughing at you because you were not able to stay upright while ice-skating? Or was it fear for your life from the violent partner that made you decide that enough was enough? Whatever the situation there was a moment in time when you said to yourself STOP! Enough is enough.

Now write down, in two columns the good things which came out of the whole situation, and the bad things which came out of it. An example of the good things may be, you found your own limits in that situation, or you found your real friends through that situation. The bad points might be things like, your self-esteem was destroyed, or you lost people and friends who were close to you because of it.

Write down as many things, good and bad as you can think of.

Now write down the answer to this question. The answer can only be either Yes or No.

Have you learned from that situation so that you will be able to deal with it in a more positive way if you were faced with it or a similar situation again?

If the answer is no then you can try to build up your confidence in yourself. The situation was tough and you probably would not like to be in it again but what if you were? Would you be ready to deal with it better this time? The worst time to have to deal with a bad situation is when you are forced into dealing with it which is usually when you are in the middle of it and when there is no other choice and the situation is imminent. If you need to make a decision at this time then you sometimes need to make a fast decision and fast decisions that are not usually well thought out can often be the wrong decisions.

Look at each of the good things on your list, which came out of the situation. Smile at yourself now and give yourself a pat on the back. I mean it, get up, go to a mirror and tell yourself well done. This might sound a bit strange but why not. It was well done. You made positive, good things come out of a bad situation. You deserve to congratulate yourself.

Now look at the bad side of the list. Beside each point write the opposite of each of the items on that list. If you can't think of the opposite then write the thing you would have liked to have felt instead of the bad thing you did feel. In other words if you felt 'let down', you might write down the word 'encouraged' beside it. In this way you can turn negative feelings and thoughts into positive ones. Now look at the new list of opposites that you have written down beside the bad thoughts list. Do you think you can change even one of these bad list items into one of the opposites?

If you can then you have won…..Well Done!

In the Workplace

Think about it. Most of us spend most of our adult life

in our workplace. There are, in my opinion few things worse than being in a job or acting in a film that does not make you happy and fulfilled or working with people who you do not get on with. Yet when we leave our last project and go to a new one we usually don't even ask ourselves what we have learned from the people we didn't enjoy working with and what the new people we will be working with will be like. Usually, we are enticed into the next project by the offer of more money or better prospects. This raises an interesting question, which we are not going to explore here but it is worth pausing to think about.

Is money more important than happiness?

Big question I think you will agree. Anyway as I said, this is not one we will think about here.

I started my working life working for a large company; one of the biggest in its field in the world. I loved it at the start. I held a managerial position and had several people answerable to me, many other people at the same level as me, and some who held a higher position than me in the company. I was dealing with the public which I know for many is a 'never again' situation, but not one of mine. My 'never again', working for this company was that I disliked the fact that the level of service I could offer the public, my customers, was directly dependant on other people. I was not in control of the service that my customers were receiving because the people above me naturally made all the important decisions and the people below me might not be doing things exactly as I would want them done. Mind you, we all think that no one is as good at doing things as well as we do them ourselves? There were also the individuals in the company's distribution factory who sometimes did not meet deadlines. This was not a huge problem for them but it was for my customers which ultimately meant it was also my problem. So, there I was, thinking that I was the best thing since sliced bread and everyone else in the company was holding me back from giving my customers the very best service. Whether this was true or not is another matter, the fact is I thought it and I vowed then never to work for a company where I was so dependant on so many other people again. What did I do? I decided, along with one of my colleagues, to start our own business. We did just that. We opened our own place and were answerable only to each other. Business decisions were made fast, our customers were happy and we were both working in an environment where we were not relying on too many other people for anything. Now comes the part where it becomes obvious that my ambition and drive overtook my fears and worries about relying on other people. You see, because we were doing our job well and because our customers were happy it meant that our small company needed to expand, take on more staff, open more outlets. Before we knew it we had almost one hundred employees. Now this might sound fantastic, a great achievement, and yes it was. We had grown the business well but I suddenly realised that I was relying on people again to give my customers a great service. So although this time around had a different angle because I was the boss, I still needed to rely on others to deliver. I had allowed myself to get into exactly the same situation as before without even realising it.

As the time came to sell the business I knew that I

wanted to do something on my own. No business partner, no staff, no bosses (I sound like a bit of a self centred hermit but I'm not) I just knew that for sixteen years I had been in jobs where I was reliant on lots of other people. I am not saying for a minute that we can do everything ourselves, that is seldom the case. We all at some time need to rely on other people in our work lives but I didn't want too many to be between myself and my customers, whether they be my bosses or my employees.

Here is the strange thing then. I had no sooner sold my company than I was being invited to co-own a business which potentially would mean I was reliant on more people than ever.

What a dilemma, what a decision I had to make. This was a chance to be in a situation that I knew I would enjoy as it was in entertainment management, which is an area I loved to be in. This fact was obviously stronger than my 'never again' fear because I went into the new situation. The thing is, it is not wrong to go into a similar situation to your 'never again', but in my opinion it is wrong if you have not dealt with why it was a never again situation in the first place and learned from it, or taken time to make sure that even if it was similar you are better equipped to deal with it this time round.

Whatever you go into in the future make sure that you go into it having fully learned from your past experiences. By doing this, you will have a much more productive and fulfilling time.

Love quotes from famous people

"Perfect love is rare indeed – for to be a love will require that you continually have the subtlety of the very wise, the flexibility of the child, the sensitivity of the artist, the understanding of the philosopher, the acceptance of the saint, the tolerance of the scholar and the fortitude of the certain."
Leo Buscaglia

"Love is a fire. But whether it is going to warm your heart or burn down your house, you can never tell."
Joan Crawford

"Gravitation cannot be held responsible for people falling in love."
Albert Einstein

"It's better to have loved and lost, than to have never loved."
Alfred Lord Tennyson

"At the touch of love, everyone becomes a poet."
Plato

"Love conquers all."
Virgil

"One word frees us of all the weight and pain in life. That word is love."
Sophocles

"LOVE: The irresistible desire to be irresistibly desired."
Mark Twain

"Love is the flower you've got to let grow."
John Lennon

"If you judge someone, you have no time to love them."
Mother Teresa

The now famous quote by Princes Diana during a television interview[I], about there being three people in her

---

[I] BBC1 Panorama interview with the Princess of Wales, broadcast in the UK in November 1995 marriage to Prince Charles does not reveal the whole truth about having a relationship played out in public. There is, in most celebrity relationships another party, who meaning to or not, plays a vital part in the relationship, the media.

For all but the most astute of high-profile people, the relationship with the media to which they unwittingly sign up, and can be more akin to a tempestuous affair than a stable relationship, has a huge impact on the couple. It not only invites the world to view the ups and downs of normal everyday life in which most of us enjoy complete privacy, but also can be the lever which comes between the couple which can eventually drive them apart.

Being in the public eye and in a relationship can be one of the most difficult things that any celebrity can do. Those people, famous or not, who want to be in a relationship, want that relationship to be built on love, trust and intimacy. For the famous this can be as tricky as building a snowman in the desert.

When a relationship crumbles the last thing the individuals involved want to do is talk about it. Coping with questions from friends can be hard enough, but pressure mounts when the world's press camp outside your house and wont leave until they can pass on to the public every detail of what went wrong.

We're only human after all; we want to know who slept with whom and whose fault it all was. But somehow our interest fades when we discover that it's something as mundane as a 'breakdown in communication' to blame.

When it comes down to it celebrity marriages are not that

different from any other except they are more public. When all the media attention fades, and the couple are left to get on with this new phase of their relationship they are basically just two people in love doing what feels right.

With what seems like more and more high-profile couples divorcing after relativity short marriages, the wedding day promise 'til death us do part' prompts questions of the couple's commitment to make the marriage a success. Although the question of whether they should have 'tried harder' is a valid one, it only serves as a smoke screen, hiding the real issue of whether they were compatible in the first place and properly equipped for the inevitable challenges that even successful marriages bring.

More and more couples, celebrity or not, seek the help of professionals when their marriage loses its sparkle; but is it too late by that time? Has the damage already been done and the gap between what each individual wants and what they are getting too wide to bridge? Sometimes not, many couples move forward and have a strong marriage after counselling. The growing awareness that when it comes to relationships, prevention is better than cure, has encouraged couples to prepare for marriage by having a coach. This can help them understand their own and their partner's needs, wants and aspirations for the future, before they tie the knot.

A common reason for marriages not lasting is lack of communication, both before the wedding and after. By exploring ways to express themselves and allowing each other to communicate freely the couple are better equipped to deal with challenges that lie ahead. They build a strong foundation based on love and trust cemented with communication and integrity.

I am pretty sure that ninety-nine couples out of a hundred will tell you that they communicate with each other verbally; but communication is much more than that. To communicate effectively sometimes you need to be silent and just listen to what your partner is saying, or more importantly, isn't saying. Listen as he or she communicates through body language and attitude, which express far more eloquently than speech ever could what is really going on. Communication before marriage or a long term committed relationship plays an important role in determining whether the relationship succeeds or not. By affording your partner the freedom to express his or her properly heard will create a benchmark for the future.

Often celebrities are in a no win situation and have difficulty finding a life partner. If they date another celebrity, egos often get in the way of romance and unhealthy competition fuels the dreaded breakdown in communication. The road is no less hazardous if the famous fall for the less famous. Parents will understand the loss of identity felt when people know them only as the mother of Susan or the father of John. It is not difficult to imagine then the pressure of being the nameless husband or wife of a world-famous star and not knowing how to communicate your feelings to your partner so that they will be heard.

Before committing to marriage those involved should ask themselves and each other why they want to spend the rest of their life with this one person. Marrying someone hoping that they will provide whatever is missing in your own life has failure written all over it. When each person takes responsibility for his or her own happiness as a fulfilled individual within the relationship, it gives the marriage a foothold. Having a loving partner should add to the happiness you already have in your life, not be the basic ingredient of what makes you happy.

Conclusion

Really, when it comes to dealing with fame and celebrity, there is not too much to say apart from hold on tight and grit your teeth.

There are very few who make it to the top in the game of celebrity and of those who do, there are only a handful for whom fame sits comfortably.

One word that springs to mind when it comes to any career, especially one that makes you a well known public figure, and that is "enjoy".

Enjoy the build up to getting the recognition that you so much desire.

Enjoy the achievement of the tasks you set yourself.

Enjoy it all when you do get it and enjoy the memories once it has gone.

Simply enjoy the journey.

Printed in Great Britain
by Amazon